# Introduction to Thai Reading

# INTRODUCTION TO
# THAI READING

Rungrat  Luanwarawat

Orchid Press

Rungrat Luanwarawat
INTRODUCTION TO THAI READING

ORCHID PRESS
P.O. Box 19,
Yuttitham Post Office,
Bangkok 10900 Thailand
*www.orchidbooks.com*

Printed in Thailand

ISBN-10: 974-524-103-2
ISBN-13: 978-974-524-103-9

# CONTENTS

# ABOUT THIS BOOK

Quite a number of Thai language learners have found that, in order to really master the Thai language, one must become adept at reading Thai.

Students who rely on books with phonetic transliterations of Thai will make limited progress. Materials with transliterated Thai face many limitations. Because there is no universal standard for transliterating Thai into English, students lose time relearning different phonetic systems. In addition, some sounds in Thai have no direct equivalent in the Roman alphabet. Even the best transliterations cannot capture all the nuances of the Thai language.

Though The Royal Institute of Thailand has issued guidelines for transliteration, Thais generally are not abiding by those guidelines and tend to create their own versions, as is evident from the many different spellings on road signs.

Learning to read Thai is the path to a more profound grasp of the language. This book is based on years of experience teaching foreigners to speak and read Thai, and builds on my observations in the classroom about which rules of grammar, spelling and pronunciation most commonly impede their progress. Those who complete it will take a substantial step towards a solid and advanced knowledge of the Thai language.

Reading Thai characters can help even advanced Thai speakers break down the words they use and thereby improve their pronunciation. For those living in Thailand or visiting frequently, knowledge of written Thai will help them understand menus, leases, street signs, advertisements and other writings which they encounter in everyday life. With the ability to read the Thai language around you, even a simple errand across town becomes a chance to expand one's knowledge of Thai vocabulary and society.

This book is suitable for students who prefer to take time in mastering the pronunciation by reading the Thai alphabet. Introduction to Thai Reading, designed to be a comprehensive foundation of 24 progressive lessons, will pave the way for higher-level learning. The book begins with an explanation of the Thai alphabet and a phonetic table listing English sounds comparable to each Thai consonant and vowel. Because Thai sounds cannot all be transliterated precisely, it is highly recommended that you rely on your ears by listening to the accompanying CD for the pronunciation of the consonants and vowels, and that you focus on the subtle differences of the five tones in particular.

When seeing the CD sign in the book, you are advised to listen to the CD and repeat afterwards. The number next to the CD sign indicates the track number.

Each lesson builds on previous lessons, so students should go through them in consecutive order. To gain the most from this book, students should not proceed to the next lesson until they can do the exercises of the preceding lesson easily and correctly. The answer keys to all exercises are provided at the end of the book.

The last section of Part 1 combines education with entertainment. Crosswords, word puzzles and other games provide enjoyable reinforcement for the preceding lessons. After completing the first part of the book, learners will be able to read and use the words they have learnt in communicating with Thai people. The second part of the book, How to Form Phrases and Sentences, explains the basic structure of the Thai language. Those who complete the book will have acquired not only essential Thai reading skills, but also the vocabulary and grammar needed for basic Thai speaking. There are thousands of useful words and literal English translations provided in this book.

# ACKNOWLEDGEMENT

I appreciate the help of my editors, Brian Pearce (Resident Legal Advisor) and L.A.J.M. Heijstee (Japanologist). Their kind contributions have been vitally important to the completion of this book. Their valuable advice will be undoubtedly of great benefit to the Thai language learners.

I also would like to thank my friends and students for their constructive comments and everlasting questions. Their curiosity and interest in Thai has encouraged me to design the language lessons appealing, enjoyable and easy to understand.

Special thanks to my friend Brett Raudenbush for his kind assistance and useful advice on the CD recording project.

# PART 1

# LESSON 1: INTRODUCTION

The Thai alphabet was formally recognized during the reign of King Ramkhamhaeng the Great (A.D. 1279-1299), the third King of the Sukhothai Kingdom. Apart from adapting the Thai alphabets from many existing sources including ancient Khmer and Mon, more consonants, vowels and tone marks were also added, so that all sounds could be written. Since then, the Thai scripts and orthography have gradually been adapted over time.

Most Thai words are monosyllabic words. Many of the disyllabic and polysyllabic words are formed by combining two or more monosyllabic words. Generally, a monosyllabic word consists of one or two initial consonants, a vowel and a tone. Some words may have final consonant(s) at the end. Should there be more than one final consonant, the final sound is always pronounced once. Usually, the final consonant which comes right after the vowel is the pronounced sound. For instance, the loan word 'lift' in English is always pronounced as 'lif' in Thai. More complicated words may have extra marks or signs attached. Readers will find those signs and explanations about their usage later in this book.

Thais have incorporated many loan words from Pali, Sanskrit, Khmer, English and Chinese into their language. Over time, some of these words have changed in sounds, tones, spellings, connotations and sometimes even meanings. The loan words, especially from English, also introduced new grammar and unprecedented final sounds (like x, s, l, etc.) to the modern Thai language.

Some Thai consonants are mainly used to write those loan words. This is one explanation why the consonant scripts (44) outnumber the consonant sounds (21).

Thai is a tonal language, meaning a different tone creates a different meaning. There are five tone sounds but four tone marks. What influences the tone sound is not only the tone mark but the combination of initial consonant(s), vowel, final consonant(s) together with the tone mark.

The Thai language does not have inflection, meaning no change of words to point out tense or number as in English. Time of action is indicated by adding extra words.

A Thai word may have several meanings and/or functions depending on its location in the sentence. The sentence structure, both in statement and question, usually starts with Subject, then Verb and Object or Modifier. For example: 'I play football'; 'I' is Subject, 'play' is Verb and 'football' is Object.

Word order in a phrase that has an adjective to qualify a noun is different from the English structure. In Thai, the adjective always follows the noun it qualifies. For example: 'clear water' in English is 'water clear' in Thai. Details of the Thai grammar are discussed in Part 2, Lesson 24.

Part 1 covers introduction of the Thai consonants, vowels and tones, and how they form words. It also highlights the major special Thai symbols and their usage. A variety of practical vocabulary lists are included at the end of this part.

# LESSON 2: CONSONANTS

There are 44 consonants in the Thai language. Their sounds depend on, among other things, the location of the consonant in the word. Some consonants have the same initial sound and some have the same final sound. A consonant's initial sound may be the same as, or differ from, its final sound. Among the 44 consonants, there are only 21 different initial sounds and 8 different final sounds.

In order to distinguish them from one another, they have all been given names. This is a long-standing system that Thai schools use in teaching their students.

There is no alphabetical order which includes both consonants and vowels as in English. Thus, each has to be learned independently.

Writing is from left to right. Learning to write a consonant or a vowel, one should start with the little circle, if any. There are no capital letters and no spaces between words; however, a break is inserted between groups of words or sentences.

The following list shows in which order Thai children learn the Thai consonants. Listen to the CD and repeat after each consonant sound. After completing the list, pronounce each consonant by yourself and check with the CD if your pronunciation is correct. ⊙ (1)

| | | | |
|---|---|---|---|
| 1. | ก | ไก่ | gaw gài | *chicken* |
| 2. | ข | ไข่ | kǎw kài | *egg* |
| 3. | ฃ | ฃวด | kǎw kùat | *bottle* [1] |

| | | | |
|---|---|---|---|
| 4. | ค | ควาย | kaw kwah-ii | *buffalo* |
| 5. | ฅ | ฅน | kaw kohn | *person* [1] |
| 6. | ฆ | ระฆัง | kaw ráh-kahng | *bell* |
| 7. | ง | งู | ngaw ngoo | *snake* |
| 8. | จ | จาน | jaw jahn | *plate* |
| 9. | ฉ | ฉิ่ง | chăw chìng | *small cymbals* |
| 10. | ช | ช้าง | chaw cháhng | *elephant* |
| 11. | ซ | โซ่ | saw sôh | *chain* |
| 12. | ฌ | เฌอ | chaw che(r) | *a kind of tree* |
| 13. | ญ | หญิง | yaw yĭng | *female* |
| 14. | ฎ | ชฎา | daw chah-dah | *traditional head dress* |
| 15. | ฏ | ปฏัก | dtaw bpàh-dtàhk | *a spiked stick used for urging cattle forward* |
| 16. | ฐ | ฐาน | tăw tăhn | *platform* |
| 17. | ฑ | มณโฑ | taw mohn-toh | *a character in Ramakian* [2] |
| 18. | ฒ | ผู้เฒ่า | taw pôo-tâo | *old man* |
| 19. | ณ | เณร | naw nehn | *novice* |
| 20. | ด | เด็ก | daw dèhk | *child* |
| 21. | ต | เต่า | dtaw dtào | *turtle* |
| 22. | ถ | ถุง | tăw tŏong | *bag* |
| 23. | ท | ทหาร | taw táh-hăhn | *soldier* |
| 24. | ธ | ธง | taw tohng | *flag* |

1. *These consonants are no longer used. They are now replaced by* ข *and* ค *respectively.*
2. *Thai epic influenced by the Ramayana of India.*

| 25. | น | หนู | naw nŏo | *mouse, rat* |
| 26. | บ | ใบไม้ | baw bai-máh-ii | *leaf* |
| 27. | ป | ปลา | bpaw bplah | *fish* |
| 28. | ผ | ผึ้ง | păw pêung | *bee* |
| 29. | ฝ | ฝา | făw făh | *lid* |
| 30. | พ | พาน | paw pahn | *chalice, tray* |
| 31. | ฟ | ฟัน | faw fahn | *tooth* |
| 32. | ภ | สำเภา | paw săhm-pao | *sailing ship* |
| 33. | ม | ม้า | maw máh | *horse* |
| 34. | ย | ยักษ์ | yaw yáhk | *giant* |
| 35. | ร | เรือ | raw reua | *boat* |
| 36. | ล | ลิง | law ling | *monkey* |
| 37. | ว | แหวน | waw wăen | *ring* |
| 38. | ศ | ศาลา | săw săh-lah | *pavilion* |
| 39. | ษ | ฤๅษี | săw reu-sĭi | *hermit* |
| 40. | ส | เสือ | săw sĕua | *tiger* |
| 41. | ห | หีบ | hăw hìip | *trunk/box* |
| 42. | ฬ | จุฬา | law jòo-lah | *a kind of kite* |
| 43. | อ | อ่าง | aw àhng | *basin, tub* |
| 44. | ฮ | นกฮูก | haw nóhk hôok | *owl* |

| | | | | | | | | | | | |
|---|---|---|---|---|---|---|---|---|---|---|---|
| ก | ก | ก | ก | ก | ก | | ข | ข | บ | ข | ข | บ |
| ค | ค | ค | ค | ค | ค | | ฆ | ฆ | ฆ | ฆ | ฆ | บ |
| ง | ง | ง | ง | ง | ง | | จ | จ | จ | จ | จ | จ |
| ฉ | ฉ | ฉ | ฉ | ฉ | ฉ | | ช | ช | ช | ช | ช | ช |
| ซ | ซ | ซ | ซ | ซ | ซ | | ฌ | ฌ | ฌ | ฌ | ฌ | ฌ |
| ญ | ญ | ญ | ญ | ญ | ญ | | ฎ | ฎ | ฎ | ฎ | ฎ | ฎ |
| ฏ | ฏ | ฏ | ฏ | ฏ | ฏ | | ฐ | ฐ | ฐ | ฐ | ฐ | ฐ |
| ฑ | ฑ | ฑ | ฑ | ฑ | ฑ | | ฒ | ฒ | ฒ | ฒ | ฒ | ฒ |
| ณ | ณ | ณ | ณ | ณ | ณ | | ด | ด | ด | ด | ด | ด |
| ต | ต | ต | ต | ต | ต | | ถ | ถ | ถ | ถ | ถ | ถ |
| ท | ท | ท | ท | ท | ท | | ธ | ธ | ธ | ธ | ธ | ธ |
| น | น | น | น | น | น | | บ | บ | บ | บ | บ | บ |
| ป | ป | ป | ป | ป | บ | | ผ | ผ | ผ | ผ | ผ | ผ |
| ฝ | ฝ | ฝ | ฝ | ฝ | ฝ | | พ | พ | พ | พ | พ | พ |
| ฟ | ฟ | ฟ | ฟ | ฟ | ฟ | | ภ | ภ | ภ | ภ | ภ | ภ |
| ม | ม | ม | ม | ม | ม | | ย | ย | ย | ย | ย | ย |
| ร | ร | ร | ร | ร | ร | | ล | ล | ล | ล | ล | ล |
| ว | ว | ว | ว | ว | ว | | ศ | ศ | ศ | ศ | ศ | ศ |
| ษ | ษ | ษ | ษ | ษ | ษ | | ส | ส | ส | ส | ส | ส |
| ห | ห | ห | ห | ห | ห | | ฬ | ฬ | ฬ | ฬ | ฬ | ฬ |
| อ | อ | อ | อ | อ | อ | | ฮ | ฮ | ฮ | ฮ | ฮ | ฮ |

Samples of different Thai fonts

The table below shows the 42 Thai consonants (the 2 obsolete consonants are not included here) and their comparable English sounds. In total, there are 21 initial consonant sounds. A Thai word may have more than one initial consonant, words with two inital consonants are further discussed in Lesson 10. While viewing the consonants, the reader is advised to listen to the CD and repeatedly pronounce them along with the speaker until you recognize the scripts and sounds. (2)

| Initial Consonants | Comparable Sounds |
|---|---|
| 1. ก | g   (as in 'go') |
| 2. ข  ค  ฆ | k |
| 3. ง | ng  (as in 'singing') |
| 4. จ | j   (as in 'jar') |
| 5. ช  ฌ  ฌ | ch |
| 6. ซ  ส  ษ  ศ | s |
| 7. ย  ญ | y   (as in 'year') |
| 8. ด  ฎ | d |
| 9. ต  ฏ | dt  (pronounced together  with the tongue touching the front teeth as with the 't' in 'stand') |
| 10. ท  ฒ  ฑ  ธ  ถ  ฐ | t   (as in 'tea') |
| 11. น  ณ | n |

| 12. บ | b |
|---|---|
| 13. ป | bp  (pronounced with the lips pursed together  as with the 'p' in 'spy') |
| 14. พ  ภ  ฬ | p  (as in 'pie') |
| 15. ฟ  ฝ | f |
| 16. ม | m |
| 17. ร | r [3] |
| 18. ล  ฬ | l |
| 19. ว | w |
| 20. ห  ฮ | h  (as in 'how') |
| 21. อ | -  used when the initial sound is silent |

The Thai language's final sounds are quite limited. Positioned as a final consonant, several of the Thai consonants have the same ending sound. In total, there are only 8 final or ending sounds, much less than the initial sounds. Also, not all 42 consonants are used as a final consonant.

---

3.  In colloquial Thai language, you may hear many people read  and pronounce ร (r) as ล (l). Sometimes, they may skip pronouncing ร completely, especially when ร is a part of an initial consonant cluster.

| Final Consonants | Comparable Sounds |
|---|---|
| 1. ก ข ค ฆ | similar to the sound of 'k' or 'g' |
| 2. ง | ng |
| 3. ม | m |
| 4. ท ฑ ฒ ธ ถ ฐ จ<br>ช ษ ศ ส ซ ด ต<br>ฎ ฏ ฌ ฑ | similar to the sound of 't' or 'd' |
| 5. น ณ ญ ร ล ฬ | n |
| 6. พ ภ ฟ บ ป | similar to the sound of 'p' or 'b' |
| 7. ว | oo (as in 'boot' but pronounced shorter) |
| 8. ย | y/ii (as in 'weed' but pronounced shorter) |

Unlike English, the final sound of a Thai word is only pronounced once, even if there is more than one final consonant. Moreover, the final 'p', 't', 'k' sounds are not pronounced or released as in English. These final sounds are 'swallowed' or stopped at the end. Due to this reason, words ending with 'p' or 'b' (6) are pronounced alike. This also explains the identical ending pronunciation of the final 'k' versus 'g' (1) and 't' versus 'd' (4)

Several English final sounds; e.g. 'l', 'f', 's', 'sh', 'ch', do not exist in the Thai language. When Thais apply a loan word ending with one of those sounds, they would generally change it to one of the eight final sounds as mentioned above.

Special attention should be given to the consonants 'ว' and 'ย'. These two consonants can also function as part of a diphthong. Observe the differences in sounds shown in the Initial Consonants Table compared to the Final Consonants Table.

More details of initial consonants and final consonants are covered in Lessons 4 and 5.

## COMPREHENSION EXERCISES

**A.Write down the consonants that have the following initial sounds.**

1. g __                           2. k __ __ __

3. ng __                          4. j __

5. ch __ __ __                    6. s __ __ __ __

7. y __ __                        8. d __ __

9. dt __ __                       10. t __ __ __ __ __ __

11. n __ __                       12. b __

13. bp __                         14. p __ __ __

15. f __ __                       16. m __

17. r __                          18. l __ __

19. w __                          20. h __ __

21. silent sound __

**B. Write down the consonants that have the following final sounds.**

1. k __ __ __ __

2. t __ __ __ __ __ __ __ __ __

__ __ __ __ __ __ __ __ __

3. p __ __ __ __ __

4. m __

5. n __ __ __ __ __ __

6. ng __

7. y/ii __

8. oo __

## LISTENING EXERCISES

**C. Listen to the CD and choose the words that begin with the following initial consonants.** (3)

1. a) มา          b) นา
2. a) โท          b) โต
3. a) ตี          b) ดี
4. a) แค่          b) แก
5. a) พอ          b) หอ
6. a) ฎู          b) ปู
7. a) ไป          b) ใบ
8. a) โทน          b) โดน
9. a) ดง          b) ธง
10. a) นาน          b) งาน

**D. Listen to the CD and choose the words that end with the following final consonants.** (3)

1. a) มาก          b) มาร
2. a) โทษ          b) โทน
3. a) ตีบ          b) ตี
4. a) แคบ          b) แคน

5. a)  พอง          b)  พอก

6. a)  ปูก           b)  ปูด

7. a)  ปาด          b)  ปาก

8. a)  ทน           b)  ทด

9. a)  ดง           b)  ดม

10. a) งาม          b)  งาน

# LESSON 3: VOWELS

There are 32 vowels which can be divided into 3 groups; monophthong (short
& long vowels), diphthong (short & long vowels) and extra vowels. Some of
the vowels are obsolete or rarely used.

A vowel cannot stand alone; it must affix to at least one consonant. The
table below shows the position of each different vowel. An underscore ( _ )
indicates the position of the initial consonant.

Vowels, written either in front of, after, above, under or all around the
consonants, are pronounced after the initial consonant(s). While viewing the
vowels, the reader is advised to listen to the CD and repeatedly pronounce
them along with the speaker until you recognize the scripts and sounds.

(4)

| Monophthong | |
|---|---|
| Short Vowels | Long Vowels |
| 1. _ะ  as in 'ma' (mother) but pronounced short | 2. _า  as in 'ma' (mother) |
| 3. _ิ  as in 'tea' but pronounced short | 4. _ี  as in 'tea' |
| 5. _ึ  like 'eu' pronounced short from your throat, like when you have a hick-up | 6. _ือ  pronounced like _ึ, but longer |

| | |
|---|---|
| 7. ◌ (placed below a consonant) sounds like 'o' in 'two', but short | 8. ◌ (placed below a consonant) sounds like 'o' in 'two' |
| 9. เ◌ะ like 'ay' in 'May' but short | 10. เ◌ like 'ay' in 'May' |
| 11. แ◌ะ like 'ai' in 'air' but short | 12. แ◌ like 'ai' in 'air' |
| 13. โ◌ะ like 'o' in 'so' but short | 14. โ◌ like 'o' in 'so' |
| 15. เ◌าะ like 'aw' in 'saw' but short | 16. ◌อ like 'aw' in 'saw' |
| 17. เ◌อะ (rarely used) like 'ir' in 'Sir' but short and with silent 'r' | 18. เ◌อ similar to 'ir' in 'Sir' but with silent 'r' |

| Diphthong | |
|---|---|
| **Short Vowels** | **Long Vowels** |
| 19. เ◌ียะ (rarely used) like 'ear' in 'year' but short with silent 'r' | 20. เ◌ีย like 'ear' in 'year' but with silent 'r' |
| 21. ◌ัวะ (rarely used) sounds like a combination of ◌ and ◌ะ | 22. ◌ัว sounds like a combination of ◌ and ◌า |

| | |
|---|---|
| 23. เ◌ือะ (rarely used) sounds like a combination of ◌ื and ◌ะ | 24. เ◌ือ sounds like a combination of ◌ื and ◌า |

| Extra Vowels | |
|---|---|
| 25. ◌ํา like 'u' in 'gum' | 26. ไ◌ like 'ai' in 'Thai' |
| 27. ใ◌ [4] like 'ai' in 'Thai' | 28. เ◌า like 'ou' in out', with silent 't' |
| 29. ฤ sounds like ริ | 30. ฤๅ sounds like รือ This vowel is no longer used. |
| 31. ฦ sounds like ลิ This vowel is no longer used. | 32. ฦๅ sounds like ลือ This vowel is no longer used. |

4. ใ◌ *only appears in 20 Thai words, which are listed in Lesson 17.*

Samples of different Thai fonts

When followed by a final consonant, some vowels change their form(s) or disappear completely while the sounds remain unchanged. Those are:

1. _ะ → _ ̆ _   Ex: ก + _ะ + บ   = กับ *(with, and)*

2. โ_ะ → _ _   Ex: ค + โ_ะ + น   = คน *(person, people)*

3. ื_อ → ื_ _   Ex: ย + ื_อ + น   = ยืน *(to stand)*

4. เ_ะ → เ ็ _ _   Ex: ล + เ_ะ + ก   = เล็ก *(small)*

5. แ_ะ → แ ็ _ _   Ex: ข + แ_ะ + ง   = แข็ง *(hard, not soft)*

6. เ_อ → เ ̂ _ _ [5]   Ex: ด + เ_อ + น   = เดิน *(to walk)*

7. _ ̆ว → _ว_   Ex: น + _ ̆ว + ด   = นวด *(to massage)*

There are some vowels that can not be followed by a final consonant when forming a word. These are '_ำ', 'เ_า' and 'ใ_'.

---

5. *Exceptions: some loan words, like:* เทอม *(term).*

# WRITING EXERCISE

Write down each of the vowels 10 times and pronounce them aloud.

1. _ะ   __   __   __   __   __   __   __   __   __   __

2. _า   __   __   __   __   __   __   __   __   __   __

3. _ิ   __   __   __   __   __   __   __   __   __   __

4. _ี   __   __   __   __   __   __   __   __   __   __

5. _ึ   __   __   __   __   __   __   __   __   __   __

6. _ือ   __   __   __   __   __   __   __   __   __   __

7. _ุ   __   __   __   __   __   __   __   __   __   __

8. _ู   __   __   __   __   __   __   __   __   __   __

9. เ_ะ   __   __   __   __   __   __   __   __   __   __

10. เ_   __   __   __   __   __   __   __   __   __   __

11. แ_ะ   __   __   __   __   __   __   __   __   __   __

12. แ_ __ __ __ __ __ __ __ __ __ __

13. ใ_ะ __ __ __ __ __ __ __ __ __ __

14. ไ_ __ __ __ __ __ __ __ __ __ __

15. ไ_ __ __ __ __ __ __ __ __ __ __

16. ใ_ __ __ __ __ __ __ __ __ __ __

17. เ_า __ __ __ __ __ __ __ __ __ __

# HOW TO READ A MONOSYLLABIC WORD

## (Tones will be mentioned in Lesson 6)

1. Pronounce the initial consonant first [6]

2. Then the vowel and

3. Finish with the final consonant, if any. (5)

| Initial Consonant | Vowel | Final Consonant | Word | |
|---|---|---|---|---|
| 1. จ | _ะ | | จะ | *will* |
| 2. ร | _ะ | ก | รัก | *to love* |
| 3. ม | _า | | มา | *to come* |
| 4. ส | ◌ี | | สี | *color* |
| 5. ผ | ◌ี | | ผี | *ghost* |
| 6. ฝ | ◌ี | ก | ฝึก | *to practice* |
| 7. ม | ◌ือ | | มือ | *hand* |
| 8. ม | ◌ือ | ด | มืด | *dark* |
| 9. ด | ◌ุ | | ดุ | *strict* |
| 10. ง | ◌ู | | งู | *snake* |
| 11. ต | เ_ะ | | เตะ | *to kick* |
| 12. ต | เ_ะ | ม | เต็ม | *full* |

6. *In the case of two initial consonants, see details in Lesson 10.*

| 13. ล | เ_ | ข | เลข *number* |
|---|---|---|---|
| 14. ล | แ_ะ | | และ *and* |
| 15. ข | แ_ะ | ง | แข็ง *hard* |
| 16. พ | แ_ | ง | แพง *expensive* |
| 17. ก | โ_ะ | ด | กด *to press* |
| 18. ต | โ_ | | โต *big* |
| 19. ก | เ_าะ | | เกาะ *island* |
| 20. จ | _อ | ด | จอด *to park* |
| 21. ป | เ_อ | ด | เปิด *to open /to turn on* |
| 22. ธ | เ_อ | | เธอ *you, her* |
| 23. ร | เ_ีย | น | เรียน *to study* |
| 24. ต | _ัว | | ตัว *body* |
| 25. ข | _ัว | ด | ขวด *bottle* |
| 26. ร | เ_ือ | | เรือ *boat* |
| 27. ท | _ำ | | ทำ *to do* |
| 28. ป | ไ_ | | ไป *to go* |
| 29. น | ใ_ | | ใน *in* |
| 30. บ | เ_า | | เบา *light /not heavy* |

## COMPREHENSION EXERCISES

### A. Which vowels

1. are placed above an initial consonant?

_____

2. are placed underneath an initial consonant?

_____

3. are placed in front of an initial consonant?

_____

4. are placed behind an initial consonant?

_____

5. are placed in front of and behind an initial consonant?

_____

6. are placed on top of and behind an initial consonant?

_____

7. change their form(s) when followed by a final consonant?

_____

## B. Find the vowels in the following words and pronounce them aloud.

1. เล็ก    *small*
2. เลข    *number*
3. ทำ    *to do, to make*
4. ดี    *good*
5. จะ    *will (future particle)*
6. ติด    *to stick, stuck*
7. ดู    *to look at, to watch*
8. มือ    *hand*
9. ทุก    *every*
10. จาก    *from*
11. ไป    *to go*
12. ใบ    *leaf*
13. โต    *big*
14. และ    *and*
15. แยก    *to separate*
16. เมือง    *town*
17. ตัว    *body (classifier)*
18. โลก    *the world*
19. เดิน    *to walk*
20. ดึก    *late at night*
21. ขวด    *bottle*
22. เจอ    *to meet*
23. เกาะ    *island*
24. สด    *fresh*
25. เรียน    *to study*
26. เอา    *to want, to get*
27. เถอะ    *urging particle*
28. เกิด    *to be born*
29. กิน    *to eat*
30. ด้วย    *too*
31. จอง    *to reserve*
32. เขียน    *to write*
33. เรา    *we*
34. น้ำ    *water*
35. มัน    *it*
36. กลัว    *to be afraid*
37. หนึ่ง    *one*
38. สอง    *two*
39. เจ็ด    *seven*
40. วัว    *cow*

## C. Name the initial consonant, vowel and final consonant (if any).

| Word | Initial Consonant | Vowel | Final Consonant |
|---|---|---|---|
| เดือน<br>*month* | | | |
| วัน<br>*day* | | | |
| ปี<br>*year* | | | |
| นาน<br>*long time* | | | |
| เห็น<br>*to see* | | | |
| รวม<br>*to include* | | | |
| หัว<br>*head* | | | |
| เดิน<br>*to walk* | | | |
| บน<br>*on* | | | |
| บอก<br>*to tell* | | | |

| เขียน<br>*to write* | | |
|---|---|---|
| อ่าน<br>*to read* | | |

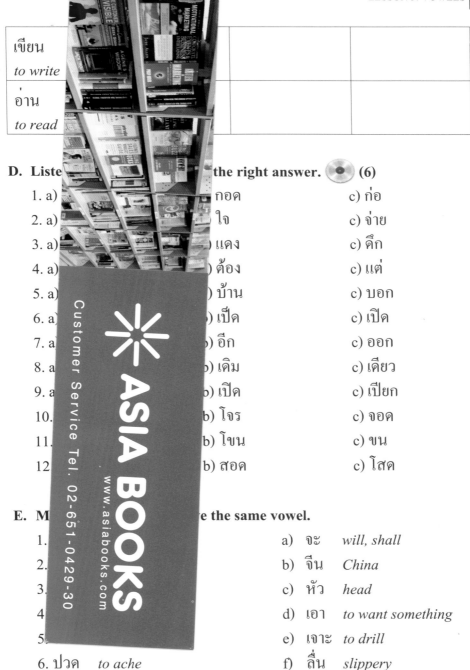

**D.** Liste the right answer. (6)

1. a)  กอด  c) ก่อ
2. a)  ใจ  c) จ่าย
3. a)  แดง  c) ดึก
4. a)  ต้อง  c) แต่
5. a)  บ้าน  c) บอก
6. a)  เป็ด  c) เปิด
7. a)  อีก  c) ออก
8. a)  เดิม  c) เดียว
9. a)  เปิด  c) เปียก
10.  b) โจร  c) จอด
11.  b) โขน  c) ขน
12.  b) สอด  c) โสด

**E.** M the same vowel.

1.
2.
3.
4.
5.
6. ปวด  *to ache*

a) จะ  *will, shall*
b) จีน  *China*
c) หัว  *head*
d) เอา  *to want something*
e) เจาะ  *to drill*
f) ลื่น  *slippery*

| | | | | | |
|---|---|---|---|---|---|
| 7. เดือน | *month* | | g) | ยุ่ง | *busy* |
| 8. ดำ | *black* | | h) | โต๊ะ | *table* |
| 9. ปี | *year* | | i) | มาก | *a lot* |
| 10. ตื่น | *to wake up* | | j) | แต่ | *but* |
| 11. ดุ | *strict, fierce* | | k) | พอ | *enough* |
| 12. แปด | *eight* | | l) | ไป | *to go* |
| 13. เก้า | *nine* | | m) | จำ | *to remember* |
| 14. เกาะ | *island* | | n) | เพื่อ | *for* |

**F. In the following article, there are five _ ะ, nine _า, two -ฺ , one -ฺ , two ไ_, one แ_ะ, two แ_ , one เ _ า, seven โ_ะ, two เ_อ, one _อ, two _า, two เ_อ, one เ_ย, one _ี, six _ี, two เ_, two _อ, two _ว. Find out where they are and write down the relevant words.**

ผม ชื่อ ดำ ผม เกิด ที่ ประเทศ ลาว ครอบครัว ผม ย้าย มา อยู่ ที่ เมือง ไทย ตั้ง แต่ ผม อายุ เก้า ขวบ ตอนนี้ ผม อายุ ยี่ สิบ สาม ปี แล้ว ผม เพิ่ง เรียน จบ และ จะ กลับ ไป ทำงาน ที่ ประเทศ ลาว เดือน หน้า

1. _ะ  _____  _____  _____  _____  _____

2. _า  _____  _____  _____  _____  _____  _____  _____

_____  _____

3. ฺ  _____  _____

4. ◌ֺ◌ุ    _____

5. ไ◌    _____    _____

6. แ◌ะ    _____

7. แ◌    _____    _____

8. เ◌า    _____

9. โ◌ะ    _____    _____    _____    _____    _____    _____

10. เ◌ือ    _____    _____

11. ◌ือ    _____

12. ◌ำ    _____    _____

13. เ◌อ    _____    _____

14. เ◌ีย    _____

15. ◌ั    _____

16. ◌ี    _____    _____    _____    _____    _____    _____

17. เ_ _____ _____

18. _อ _____ _____

19. ัว _____ _____

# LESSON 4: Initial Consonants

We have learnt all individual consonants and vowels and seen the differences between short and long vowels, diphthongs and extra vowels. This lesson will cover the classification of initial consonants, followed by lessons on final consonants and tone marks.

In Thai, words that sound alike, but have different tones, will have different meanings. There are four key factors influencing the tone:
1. Initial Consonant's Class
2. Vowel Groups
3. Final Consonant's Class
4. Tone Mark

## Initial Consonant Classification

Most Thai language books divide the initial consonants into three classes, but with two sub-groups in Class 3. This classification into three classes called middle, high and low class consonants is often found to be misleading for Thai language learners. To avoid the confusion, this book divides initial consonants into four classes instead. Consonants in the same class follow the same tone rules. The bracketed consonants have the same sound and tone as the preceding consonants. The consonants in Class 2 and Class 3 also have the same sounds but differ in tone.

Initial Class 1 includes:

| | | | | | | |
|---|---|---|---|---|---|---|
| ก | จ | ด (ฎ) | ต (ฏ) | บ | ป | อ |

INITIAL CLASS 2  includes all 10 rising-tone consonants:[7]

ข   ฉ   ถ (ฐ)   ผ   ฝ   ส (ศ, ษ)   ห

INITIAL CLASS 3 consonants sound like the ones in Class 2 but differ in tone: [7]

ค (ฆ)   ช (ฌ)   ท (ธ, ฑ, ฒ)   พ (ภ)   ฟ   ซ   ฮ

INITIAL CLASS 4  includes:

ง   ย (ญ)   น (ณ)   ร   ล (ฬ)   ว   ม

**Compare the sounds of Class 2 with Class 3.**  (7)

| Class 2 | | Class 3 | |
|---|---|---|---|
| ข | = | ค , ฆ | (k) |
| ฉ | = | ช , ฌ | (ch) |
| ถ, ฐ | = | ท, ธ, ฑ, ฒ | (t) |
| ผ | = | พ, ภ | (p) |
| ฝ | = | ฟ | (f) |
| ส, ศ, ษ | = | ซ | (s) |
| ห | = | ฮ | (h) |

_7. See comparison after Initial Class 4._

## WRITING EXERCISE

**Write down each of the consonants 10 times and pronounce them aloud.**

### CLASS 1

ก   ___   ___   ___   ___   ___   ___   ___   ___   ___   ___

จ   ___   ___   ___   ___   ___   ___   ___   ___   ___   ___

ด   ___   ___   ___   ___   ___   ___   ___   ___   ___   ___

ต   ___   ___   ___   ___   ___   ___   ___   ___   ___   ___

ฎ   ___   ___   ___   ___   ___   ___   ___   ___   ___   ___

ฏ   ___   ___   ___   ___   ___   ___   ___   ___   ___   ___

บ   ___   ___   ___   ___   ___   ___   ___   ___   ___   ___

ป   ___   ___   ___   ___   ___   ___   ___   ___   ___   ___

อ   ___   ___   ___   ___   ___   ___   ___   ___   ___   ___

### CLASS 2

ข   ___   ___   ___   ___   ___   ___   ___   ___   ___   ___

ฉ   ___   ___   ___   ___   ___   ___   ___   ___   ___   ___

ถ   ___   ___   ___   ___   ___   ___   ___   ___   ___   ___

ฐ   ___   ___   ___   ___   ___   ___   ___   ___   ___   ___

ผ   ___   ___   ___   ___   ___   ___   ___   ___   ___   ___

ฝ   ___   ___   ___   ___   ___   ___   ___   ___   ___   ___

ส   ___   ___   ___   ___   ___   ___   ___   ___   ___   ___

ศ   ___   ___   ___   ___   ___   ___   ___   ___   ___   ___

ษ   ___   ___   ___   ___   ___   ___   ___   ___   ___   ___

ห   ___   ___   ___   ___   ___   ___   ___   ___   ___   ___

## CLASS 3

ค   ___   ___   ___ ___   ___   ___   ___   ___

ฆ   ___   ___   ___   ___   ___   ___   ___   ___

ช   ___   ___   ___   ___   ___   ___   ___   ___

ฌ   ___   ___   ___   ___   ___   ___   ___   ___

ท   ___   ___   ___   ___   ___   ___   ___   ___

ธ   ___   ___   ___   ___   ___   ___   ___   ___

ฑ   ___   ___   ___   ___   ___   ___   ___   ___

ฒ   ___   ___   ___   ___   ___   ___   ___   ___

พ   ___   ___   ___   ___   ___   ___   ___   ___

ภ   ___   ___   ___   ___   ___   ___   ___   ___

ฟ   ___   ___   ___   ___   ___   ___   ___   ___

ฌ   ___   ___   ___   ___   ___   ___   ___   ___

ฮ   ___   ___   ___   ___   ___   ___   ___   ___

## CLASS 4

ง   ___   ___   ___   ___   ___   ___   ___   ___

ย   ___   ___   ___   ___   ___   ___   ___   ___

ญ   ___   ___   ___   ___   ___   ___   ___   ___

น   ___   ___   ___   ___   ___   ___   ___   ___

ณ   ___   ___   ___   ___   ___   ___   ___   ___

ร   ___   ___   ___   ___   ___   ___   ___   ___

ล   ___   ___   ___   ___   ___   ___   ___   ___

ฬ   ___   ___   ___   ___   ___   ___   ___   ___

ว   ___   ___   ___   ___   ___   ___   ___   ___

ม   ___   ___   ___   ___   ___   ___   ___   ___

# COMPREHENSION EXERCISES

## A 1. Which consonants below are not in Class 1?

| | | | | |
|---|---|---|---|---|
| ฏ | ข | บ | จ | ค |
| ฎ | ย | ฟ | ศ | ค |
| ป | อ | ต | ก | ท |

## A 2. Which consonants below are not in Class 2?

| | | | | |
|---|---|---|---|---|
| ม | ข | ฐ | ร | ผ |
| ศ | ห | ษ | จ | พ |
| ว | ฉ | ถ | ผ | ส |

## A 3. Which consonants below are not in Class 3?

| | | | | |
|---|---|---|---|---|
| ค | ฆ | ล | ช | ฌ |
| ท | ฮ | ฑ | ฒ | ภ |
| ซ | อ | ฟ | พ | ธ |

## A 4. Which consonants below are not in Class 4?

| | | | | |
|---|---|---|---|---|
| ย | ง | ญ | น | ล |
| ณ | ร | พ | ว | ม |

## B. Match the consonants that share the same sound and tone.

| | | | |
|---|---|---|---|
| 1. | ธ | A. | ท |
| 2. | ญ | B. | ษ |
| 3. | ถ | C. | ค |

| 4. | น | D. | ย |
|---|---|---|---|
| 5. | ต | E. | ณ |
| 6. | ส | F. | ฐ |
| 7. | ฎ | G. | ฏ |

## C. Match the equivalent sounds of the consonants from Class 2 (rising tone) on the left with the consonants from Class 3 on the right.

| Class 2 | | Class 3 | |
|---|---|---|---|
| 1. | ข | A. | ท |
| 2. | ฉ | B. | ฟ |
| 3. | ถ | C. | ซ |
| 4. | ผ | D. | พ |
| 5. | ฝ | E. | ช |
| 6. | ส | F. | ฮ |
| 7. | ห | G. | ค |

# LESSON 5: Final Consonants

As mentioned in Lesson 2, there are only 8 final consonant sounds in the Thai language. This lesson will cover the classification of final consonants. Consonants in the same class follow the same rules of tone.

## Final Consonant Classification

Final Consonants can be divided mainly into two classes; Sonorant Final and Stop Final. Each class is divided into subgroups, consisting of one or more consonants.

## Sonorant Final Class includes:

1. The 'ง' final sound

2. The 'ม' final sound

3. The 'น' final sound
   Consonants น, ณ, ญ, ร, ล, ฬ have the 'น' final sound.

4. The 'ย' final sound

5. The 'ว' final sound

**STOP FINAL CLASS INCLUDES:**

6. The 'ก' final sound

Consonants ก, ข, ค, ฆ have the 'ก' final sound.

7. The ' ด ' final sound

Consonants ด, ฎ, จ, ฉ, ช, ฌ, ซ, ฐ, ฑ,
ต, ฏ, ท, ธ, ฒ, ษ, ศ, ส have the ' ด '
final sound.

8. The ' บ ' final sound

Consonants บ, ป, พ, ภ, ฟ have the ' บ ' final sound.

## COMPREHENSION EXERCISES

**A. Write down the 10 Sonorant Final Consonants and pronounce
them aloud.**

1. _____      2. _____

3. _____      4. _____

5. _____      6. _____

7. _____      8. _____

9. _____      10. _____

**B. Which of the consonants above have an 'n' sound?**

_____ _____ _____ _____ _____ _____

## C. Write down the Stop Final Consonants and pronounce them aloud.

1. The ก final sound

    1.1. _____             1.2. _____

    1.3. _____             1.4. _____

2. The ด final sound

    2.1. _____             2.2. _____

    2.3. _____             2.4. _____

    2.5. _____             2.6. _____

    2.7. _____             2.8. _____

    2.9. _____             2.10. _____

    2.11. _____             2.12. _____

    2.13. _____             2.14. _____

    2.15. _____             2.16. _____

    2.17. _____             2.18. _____

3. The บ final sound

    3.1. _____             3.2. _____

    3.3. _____             3.4. _____

    3.5. _____

**D. Which word in the right column is pronounced the same as the one in the left column? Choose A. or B.**

| | | |
|---|---|---|
| 1. คัน | A. คัญ | B. คัต |
| 2. ติด | A. ติท | B. ติพ |
| 3. สอบ | A. สอด | B. สอป |
| 4. มุก | A. มุท | B. มุข |
| 5. หาร | A. หาน | B. หาว |
| 6. โดด | A. โดส | B. โดม |
| 7. เทพ | A. เทบ | B. เทก |
| 8. แถบ | A. แถป | B. แถค |
| 9. จัน | A. จัล | B. จัง |
| 10. มาก | A. มาค | B. มาฒ |
| 11. ทาน | A. ทาม | B. ทาร |
| 12. ปก | A. ปธ | B. ปค |
| 13. ลิ่น | A. ลิ่ม | B. ลิ่ณ |
| 14. พุธ | A. พุท | B. พุพ |
| 15. ทัศ | A. ทัฒ | B. ทับ |

**E. Which word in the right column has the same final sound as the one in the left column? Choose A. or B.**

| | | |
|---|---|---|
| 1. คด | A. คัญ | B. คัต |
| 2. ตัด | A. ติท | B. ติพ |
| 3. สับ | A. สอด | B. สอป |
| 4. มาก | A. มุท | B. มุข |
| 5. โหร | A. หาน | B. หาว |
| 6. ดีด | A. โดส | B. โดม |
| 7. ทัพ | A. เทบ | B. เทก |
| 8. ถูก | A. แถป | B. แถค |
| 9. จีน | A. จัล | B. จัง |
| 10. มุข | A. มาค | B. มาฒ |
| 11. ทัน | A. ทาม | B. ทาร |
| 12. ปัด | A. ปีธ | B. ปีค |
| 13. โล้น | A. ลิ่ม | B. ลิ่ณ |
| 14. พูด | A. พุท | B. พุพ |
| 15. ทิศ | A. ทัส | B. ทับ |

**F. In each of the following consonant boxes, write down**

   **1. Initial sound & Class  2. Final sound & Class**

| | | | | |
|---|---|---|---|---|
| ก | ข | ค | ฆ | ง |
| จ | ฉ | ช | ซ | ฌ |
| ญ | ฎ | ฏ | ฐ | ฑ |
| ฒ | ณ | ด | ต | ถ |
| ท | ธ | น | บ | ป |
| ผ | ฝ | พ | ฟ | ภ |
| ม | ย | ร | ล | ว |
| ศ | ษ | ส | ห | ฬ |
| อ | ฮ | | | |

**G. Match each Thai word in the left column with its corresponding phonetic form in the right column.**[8]

| Thai Word | | Phonetics |
|---|---|---|
| 1. ดี | *good* | A. kàhp |
| 2. เก่ง | *skillful* | B. róht |

---

8. *The tone marks in the right column (à, â, á, ǎ) will be explained in Lesson 6.*

| 3. เรียน | to study | C. chêu |
| 4. ลูก | one's child | D. nai |
| 5. สอน | to teach | E. koon |
| 6. รถ | car | F. gèhp |
| 7. เพื่อน | friend | G. dii |
| 8. แม่ | mother | H. rian |
| 9. ห้า | five | I. jahm |
| 10. เก็บ | to keep | J. gèhng |
| 11. ชื่อ | name | K. pêuan |
| 12. จำ | to memorize | L. săwn |
| 13. ใน | in | M. hâh |
| 14. ขับ | to drive | N. mâe |
| 15. คุณ | you | O. lôok |

# LESSON 6: Tones

There are five tone sounds in the Thai language.

1. Mid tone is the normal pitch of voice.
2. Low tone goes lower than the normal pitch of voice.
3. Falling tone begins at a high pitch then goes higher and drops lower.
4. High tone goes higher than normal pitch.
5. Rising tone begins at a low pitch and then rises sharply. (8)

| Mid | Low | Falling | High | Rising |
|-----|-----|---------|------|--------|
| gah | gàh | gâh | gáh | găh |

In Thai writing, for the five tone sounds, there are only four tone marks. The scripts and names are shown in the following table. The tone mark is always placed above the initial consonant. Should there be a vowel above the initial consonant, the tone mark is placed on top of the vowel. Each tone mark does not necessarily signify a specific tone sound. Rather, a syllable's tone is derived from a combination of the initial and final consonants, the vowel and the tone mark.

| Tone Marks | ่ | ้ | ๊ | ๋ |
|------------|----|----|----|----|
| Names | ไม้เอก <br> Mái èhk | ไม้โท <br> Mái toh | ไม้ตรี <br> Mái dtrii | ไม้จัตวา <br> Mái jàht-dtah-wah |

## IMPORTANT USAGE NOTES

1. Only consonants belonging to **Initial Consonant Class 1**[9] can be combined with all of the tone marks. When a consonant from this class appears without any tone mark, it usually has mid tone or neutral pitch of voice. With the appearance of

   **◌่**

       it changes to low tone

   **◌้**

       it changes to falling tone

   **◌๊**

       it changes to high tone

   **+**

       it changes to rising tone

2. When a consonant belonging to **Initial Consonant Class 2** appears without any tone mark, it usually carries a rising tone. This group of consonants can only be combined with two tone marks. With

   **◌่**

       it changes to low tone

   **◌้**

       it changes to falling tone

3. When a consonant belonging to **Initial Consonant Class 3 or 4** appears without any tone mark, it usually carries a mid tone. Consonants from these two groups appear mostly with the following tone marks. With

---

9. *See Lesson 4 for classification of initial consonants.*

'

it changes to falling tone

_y_

it changes to high tone

4. If a **Stop Final Class**[10] consonant or a **short open vowel** appears after a consonant from **Initial Consonant Class 1 or 2**, it will create a low tone.

5. If a **Stop Final Class** consonant appears after a consonant from **Initial Consonant Class 3 or 4**, it will create a falling tone or high tone, depending on the vowel they combine with. More details are mentioned in each consonant group later in this lesson.

---

10. _See Lesson 5 for classification of final consonants._

## Combinations of Initial Consonants, Tone Marks, Vowels and Final Consonants

### 1. Initial Consonant Class 1

ก    จ    ด (ฎ)    ต (ฏ)    บ    ป    อ

| Initial Cl. 1 combined with | | RESULTING TONE | | | | |
|---|---|---|---|---|---|---|
| | | Mid | Low | Falling | High | Rising |
| a. long open vowel | | กา | ก่า | ก้า | ก๊า | ก๋า |
| b. any vowel + sonorant final | | ดิน | ดิ่น | ดิ้น | ดิ๊น | ดิ๋น |
| c. open short vowel | | - | จะ | จ้ะ | จ๊ะ | จ๋ะ |
| d. any vowel + stop final | | - | จับ | จ้บ | จ๊บ | จ๋บ |

### Vocabulary (9)

**Mid tone words:**

| จาน | ดี | ดิน | ดู | เบา |
|---|---|---|---|---|
| *plate* | *good* | *soil* | *to watch* | *light (adj.)* |

**Low tone words:**

| ไก่ | เกิด | เกาะ | กี่ | จาก |
|---|---|---|---|---|
| *chicken* | *to be born* | *island* | *how many?* | *from* |
| จีบ | จด | เด็ก | ตอบ | อีก |
| *to flirt* | *to note down* | *child* | *to answer* | *more* |

| ปวด | ออก | ปาก | จัด | แต่ |
|---|---|---|---|---|
| *ache* | *out* | *mouth* | *to arrange* | *but* |

**Falling tone words:**

| จู้จี้ | ดื้อ | ด้วย | ใต้ | ต้อง |
|---|---|---|---|---|
| *fussy* | *stubborn* | *too* | *under* | *must* |
| บ้าน | บ้า | ป้าย | อ้วน | แก้ว |
| *house* | *crazy* | *sign* | *fat* | *glass* |

**High tone words:** (There are only a few Thai words using ⁷ )

โต๊ะ

*table/desk*

**Rising tone words:** (There are only a few Thai words using ⁺ )

จุ๋มจิ๋ม

*cute, tiny (slang)*

**See notes later in this lesson.**

## COMPREHENSION EXERCISE INITIAL CONSONANT CLASS 1

**A. Identify the tones and read the words.**

| 1. เดิน | *to walk* | 2. แดง | *red* |
|---|---|---|---|
| 3. กลุ้ม | *worried* | 4. แก่ | *old (person)* |
| 5. กิน | *to eat* | 6. เก่ง | *skillful* |
| 7. กางเกง | *trousers* | 8. เดี๋ยว | *Wait!* |
| 9. ก่อน | *before, first* | 10. จำ | *to remember* |

| | | | | |
|---|---|---|---|---|
| 11. ได้ | *to be able to* | 12. อ่าน | *to read* |
| 13. ด้าน | *side* | 14. บน | *on* |
| 15. ปิด | *to close, turn off* | 16. ประตู | *door* |
| 17. เปิด | *to open, turn on* | 18. เตี้ย | *short* |
| 19. บ่น | *to complain* | 20. ตัว | *body* |
| 21. โต | *big* | 22. ปาก | *mouth* |
| 23. แตก | *shattered* | 24. อาจ | *might, may* |
| 25. บอด | *blind* | 26. ดีใจ | *glad* |
| 27. ตก | *to fall* | 28. ตุ๊กตา | *doll* |
| 29. แป้ง | *powder* | 30. แดด | *sunlight* |

## 2. Initial Consonant Class 2

ข    ฉ    ถ (ฐ)    ผ    ฝ    ส (ศ, ษ)    ห

### & Initial Consonant Class 4  preceded by  ห

(ห  is used as a silent consonant before consonants Class 4 to produce the following tones: หง  หย (หญ)  หน (หณ)  หร  หล  หว  หม)

| Initial Cl. 2 or ห+ Initial Cl. 4 combined with | RESULTING TONE | | | | |
|---|---|---|---|---|---|
| | Mid | Low | Falling | High | Rising |
| a. long open vowel | - | ข่า | ข้า | - | ขา |
| b. any vowel + sonorant final | - | หย่า | หย้า | - | หยา |
| | - | ส่อง | ส้อง | - | สอง |
| | - | หล่าย | หล้าย | - | หลาย |

| c. short open vowel | - | ขะ | ขี๊ะ[11] | - | - |
| d. any vowel + stop final | - | หมะ | หมั๊ะ[11] | - | - |
| | - | ผัก | ผั๊ก[11] | - | - |
| | - | หมด | หมั๊ด[11] | - | - |

## VOCABULARY  (10)

**Mid tone words: none**

**Low tone words:**

| ถูก | ผิด | ขาด | ผัด | หยุด |
|---|---|---|---|---|
| *correct, cheap* | *wrong* | *lack* | *stir-fried* | *stop* |
| หย่า | หน่อย | หาด | ผัก | หนัก |
| *divorce* | *a little* | *beach* | *vegetable* | *heavy* |

**Falling tone words:**

| ผ้า | ถ้า | ห้อง | หญ้า | ข้าง |
|---|---|---|---|---|
| *cloth* | *if* | *room* | *grass* | *side* |

**High tone words: none**

**Rising tone words:**

| สูง | เสียง | หวาน | หญิง | หมา |
|---|---|---|---|---|
| *high* | *sound* | *sweet* | *female* | *dog* |
| หรือ | สี | สอง | สาม | ศูนย์ |
| *or* | *color* | *two* | *three* | *zero* |

*11. These combinations are hardly seen.*

**Remark:** There are a few words in Thai including ฉัน (I), เขา (she, he) and ไหม (a question word) which are pronounced with high tone rather than rising tone indicated by the consonant class. Many publications also spell these words according to their conversational sounds: ชั้น, เค้า, มั๊ย ?

**See notes later in this lesson.**

## COMPREHENSION EXERCISE INITIAL CONSONANT CLASS 1, 2
### AND CLASS 4 PRECEDED BY ห

**B. Identify the tones and read the words / phrases.**

| | | |
|---|---|---|
| 1. ข้าว สี ขาว | | *The rice is white./ white rice* |
| 2. เดิน ผ่าน | | *to walk past* |
| 3. ฝน ตก | | *It's raining.* |
| 4. ผิว สวย | | *The skin is beautiful. / beautiful skin* |
| 5. ก๋วยเตี๋ยว | | *Thai noodle dish* |
| 6. ถือ ถุง | | *to carry a bag* |
| 7. หรือ | | *or* |
| 8. ผอม เกิน ไป | | *too thin* |
| 9. ผม สั้น | | *short hair* |
| 10. ผู้ใหญ่ | | *adult* |
| 11. ข้าว ต้ม | | *boiled rice* |
| 12. ข้าง บน | | *upstairs* |
| 13. ห้าม เดิน ผ่าน | | *No Trespassing* |
| 14. ห้อง ไหน? | | *Which room?* |
| 15. อาหาร สด | | *fresh food* |

16. เขา เป็นโสด     *He/she is single.*

17. หก เดือน     *six months*

## 3. Initial Consonant Class 3

ค (ฅ)   ช (ฌ)   ท (ธ, ฑ, ฒ)   พ (ภ)   ฟ   ซ   ฮ

### & Initial Consonant Class 4

ง   ย (ญ)   น (ณ)   ร   ล (ฬ)   ว   ม

| Initial Cl. 3 or 4 combined with | RESULTING TONE | | | | |
|---|---|---|---|---|---|
| | Mid | Low | Falling | High | Rising |
| a. long open vowel | คา | - | ค่า | ค้า | - |
| | ยา | - | ย่า | ย้า | - |
| b. any vowel + sonorant final | ทุน | - | ทุ่น | ทุ้น | - |
| | โวย | - | โว่ย | โว้ย | - |
| c. long vowel + stop final | - | - | พูด | พู้ด [12] | พู๋ด [12] |
| d. short vowel + stop final | - | - | ซิ่บ [12] | ซิบ | ซิ๋บ [12] |
| e. short open vowel | - | - | ค่ะ | คะ | ค๋ะ [12] |

12. *These combinations are hardly seen.*

## VOCABULARY 💿 (11)

**Mid tone words:**

| คอย | งาน | นอน | แพง | ใน |
|---|---|---|---|---|
| to wait | job | to sleep | expensive | in |
| ยอม | มา | พอ | รอ | เมา |
| to allow | to come | enough | to wait | drunk |
| ยืน | ยาว | เร็ว | ลง | คน |
| to stand | long | fast | to go down | person |

**Low tone words: none**

**Falling tone words:**

| ค่า | ชอบ | โชค | นั่ง | วิ่ง |
|---|---|---|---|---|
| fee | to like | luck | to sit | to run |
| ง่วง | พูด | แรก | พ่อ | ที่ |
| sleepy | to speak | the first | father | at |
| เริ่ม | รีบ | เรียก | ลูก | |
| to start | hurry | to call | one's child | |

**High tone words:**

| คิด | ช้า | ช้าง | ฟ้า | ม้า |
|---|---|---|---|---|
| to think | slow | elephant | sky | horse |
| พัก | พบ | ทุก | ร้อย | รัก |
| to rest | to meet | every | hundred | to love |

**Rising tone words: none**

**See notes later in this lesson.**

## SUMMARY TABLE OF TONES

| Initial Consonant | RESULTING TONE | | | | |
|---|---|---|---|---|---|
| | Mid | Low | Falling | High | Rising |
| **Class 1**<br>- long open vowel, any vowel with sonorant final | กา<br>กัน<br>กาน | ก่า<br>กั่น<br>ก่าน | ก้า<br>กั้น<br>ก้าน | ก๊า<br>กั๊น<br>ก๊าน | ก๋า<br>กั๋น<br>ก๋าน |
| - short open vowel, any vowel with stop final | -<br>-<br>- | กะ<br>กัด<br>กาด | ก้ะ<br>กั้ด<br>ก้าด | ก๊ะ<br>กั๊ด<br>ก๊าด | ก๋ะ<br>กั๋ด<br>ก๋าด |
| **Class 2**<br>- long open vowel, any vowel with sonorant final | -<br>-<br>- | ข่า<br>ขั่น<br>ข่าน | ข้า<br>ขั้น<br>ข้าน | -<br>-<br>- | ขา<br>ขัน<br>ขาน |
| - short open vowel, any vowel with stop final | -<br>-<br>- | ขะ<br>ขัด<br>ขาด | ข้ะ<br>ขั้ด<br>ข้าด | -<br>-<br>- | -<br>-<br>- |
| **Class 3 & 4**<br>- long open vowel, any vowel with sonorant final | คา<br>คัน<br>คาน | -<br>-<br>- | ค่า<br>คั่น<br>ค่าน | ค้า<br>คั้น<br>ค้าน | -<br>-<br>- |
| - short open vowel, any vowel with stop final | -<br>-<br>- | -<br>-<br>- | ค่ะ<br>คั่ก<br>คาก | คะ<br>คัก<br>ค้าก | ค๋ะ<br>คั๋ก<br>ค๋าก |

**Notes:**

1. Initial Consonant Classes 3 & 4 do not have low tone.

2. Initial Consonant Class 2 does not have mid and high tones.

3. Since Initial Consonant Classes 2 & 3 have matching sounds but differ in tones, they can complement each other to complete the five tones.

4. From Note No. 3, there are two ways of spelling a falling tone word. It can be spelled by either Initial Consonant Class 2 or 3. Some words are spelled with class 2 in combination with '＂' while some are spelt with class 3 in combination with '＇'

   **Examples:** ถ้า (*if*) reads the same as ท่า (*pier*), ห้อง (*room*) reads the same as ฮ่อง (*Hong from Hong Kong*). There is no clear rule stating the usage of these two combinations. Recognition of the words is the most prominent way of learning, even for Thai people.

5. Unlike Initial Consonant Class 3, Initial Consonant Class 4 does not have a matching group. To create the missing tones, you need the presence of 'ห' in front. With the 'ห' combination, the tone rules follow Initial Consonant Class 2.

   5.1 With the presence of 'ห' but without a tone mark, it creates a rising tone but a low tone when followed by a consonant from Stop Final Class.

   5.2 With the presence of '＇' above the Initial Consonant Class 4, it creates a low tone.

   5.3 There are two ways of spelling a falling tone word in Initial Consonant Class 4:
   - Some words have 'ห' in front, together with '＂' above the Initial Consonant Class 4.
   - Some do not need 'ห' in front but only '＇' above the Initial Consonant Class 4.

**Examples:** หน้า (*face*) reads the same as  น่า (*a prefix*)

หง้าย  -  reads the same as  ง่าย (*easy*)

## COMPREHENSION EXERCISES INITIAL CONSONANT
## CLASSES 1, 2, 3 & 4

**C. Identify the tones and read the words / phrases.**

1. ที่ ไหน ?  *where?*
2. บาง ครั้ง  *sometimes*
3. ภา ษา  *language*
4. วัน นี้  *today*
5. เดือน หน้า  *next month*
6. โรง หนัง  *movie theatre*
7. คิด ไม่ ออก  *can't figure out*
8. มอง ไม่ เห็น  *can't see*
9. ทุก ครั้ง  *every time*
10. ปวด ท้อง  *stomach-ache*
11. ห้าม สูบ บุหรี่  *No Smoking*
12. เมื่อ ก่อน นี้  *previously*
13. ที่ จอด รถ  *car park*
14. รถ ไฟ  *train*
15. อะไร?  *what?*
16. ไฟ ฟ้า  *electricity*
17. เมื่อ ไร?  *when?*
18. นา ฬิ กา  *clock/watch*

## D. Which two of the three Thai words in each line have the same tone?

1. a) สี
color

b) หาย
missing

c) เก็บ
to keep

2. a) แตก
shattered

b) ด้วย
also

c) หัก
broken into pieces

3. a) ร้าน
shop

b) คับ
tight

c) ทาง
way

4. a) จน
poor

b) ฝา
lid

c) ยาย
grandmother

5. a) ถ้วย
cup

b) ช่วย
to help

c) ร้าย
bad

6. a) สด
fresh

b) พา
to bring

c) ตัด
to cut

7. a) อาบ
to bathe

b) ลอง
to try

c) นอน
to sleep

8. a) หนี
to flee

b) ผอม
thin

c) อ้วน
fat

9. a) แรก
the first

b) ผ้า
cloth

c) ค้า
to trade

10. a) ร่ม
     *umbrella*
     b) ได้
     *to be able*
     c) น้ำ
     *water*

## E. Specify initial consonant, vowel, final consonant and tone of the following words.

| Words | | Initial Cons. | Vowel | Final Cons. | Tone |
|---|---|---|---|---|---|
| 1. กับ | *with* | ก | ◌ะ | บ | Low |
| 2. ยุ่ง | *busy* | | | | |
| 3. ลื่น | *slippery* | | | | |
| 4. วัด | *temple* | | | | |
| 5. เดือน | *month* | | | | |
| 6. เดิน | *to walk* | | | | |
| 7. เพื่อน | *friend* | | | | |
| 8. กิน | *to eat* | | | | |
| 9. ถูก | *cheap* | | | | |
| 10. แพง | *expensive* | | | | |
| 11. โมง | *o'clock* | | | | |
| 12. ร้าน | *shop* | | | | |
| 13. สี | *color* | | | | |
| 14. เขียน | *to write* | | | | |
| 15. น้ำ | *water* | | | | |
| 16. ด้วย | *too* | | | | |
| 17. ต้อง | *must* | | | | |

## READING EXERCISE

| ผม | เป็น | คน | ไทย |
|---|---|---|---|
| *I* | *am* | *people/person* | *Thai* |
| เกิด | ที่ | จังหวัด | เชียงใหม่ |
| *born* | *at* | *province* | *Chiang Mai* |
| มี | พี่ชาย | สอง | คน |
| *have* | *older brother* | *two* | *persons* |
| คุณพ่อ | เป็น | หมอ | |
| *father* | *to be* | *doctor* | |
| คุณแม่ | เป็น | ครู | |
| *mother* | *to be* | *teacher* | |

*I am Thai. I was born in Chiang Mai. I have 2 older brothers. My father is a doctor. My mother is a teacher.*

| ฉัน | มา | จาก | จีน |
|---|---|---|---|
| *I* | *come* | *from* | *China* |
| ฉัน | ชอบ | อาหาร | ไทย |
| *I* | *like* | *food* | *Thai* |
| แต่ | ทาน | เผ็ด | ไม่ได้ |
| *but* | *eat* | *spicy* | *cannot* |

*I come from China. I like Thai food but I can't eat spicy food.*

# LESSON 7: THE KEY FOUR 'อ' WORDS

There are four words where ' อ ' is used as a silent consonant before ' ย '. They are:

| | |
|---|---|
| อย่า | Don't...! |
| อยู่ | to stay, to live, to be located |
| อย่าง | kind, type |
| อยาก | to want, to wish |

All of them have low tone.

**Examples:**

| | |
|---|---|
| อย่าไป! | *Don't go!* |
| ห้องน้ำอยู่ที่ไหน? | *Where is the toilet?* |
| มีอาหารสามอย่าง | *There are three kinds of food.* |
| ผมอยากนอน | *I want to sleep.* |

# LESSON 8: How to Read Groups of Words

In written Thai language, there are no capital letters and no spaces between words as in English. This lesson provides guidelines, examples and exercises, for breaking sentences into individual words, making Thai easier to read.

**Guidelines:**

1.  Observe the position of the vowels. Some vowels are always at the beginning of a word, some are above the initial consonant, some are below, some are behind and some are around the initial consonant. In case of two initial consonants, the vowel, if any, is always placed above or below the second consonant.

2.  Observe the position of the tone mark which is placed above the initial consonant of a word. In the case of two initial consonants, the tone mark, if any, is placed above the second consonant.

3.  Determine whether the vowel is of the kind that cannot stand alone, but needs a final consonant.

4.  Try to read and see if it is understandable. (This might be challenging as you need to know enough vocabulary to be able to recognize the meaning of a word.)

5.  Look for the ' ੖ ' sign, which usually stands at the end of a word. The consonant below the ' ੖ ' sign is not pronounced. For more details, see Lesson 13: Miscellaneous Signs.

The following examples (A & B) show you how to analyze a phrase step by step according to the guidelines above. Example C shows you how to analyze a phrase word by word based on the explanation shown in the guidelines.

**Example A:** บ้านสีขาว (*The house is white.*)

    1.  า (บ้าน, ขาว) comes after the initial consonant.

        ี (สี) is above the initial consonant.

    2.  ้ (บ้าน) comes above the initial consonant.

    3.  า and ี may or may not be followed by a final consonant.

        น may be the final consonant of บ้า or the first initial

        consonant of สี (in case of two initial consonants).

    4.  บ้า-นสี-ขาว makes no sense but บ้าน-สี-ขาว means 'a white house'.

    5.  no ์ sign.

**Example B:** ชอบกินเผ็ด (*Like to eat spicy.*)

    1.  อ (ชอบ) as a vowel comes after the initial consonant.

        ิ (กิน) is above the initial consonant.

        เ็ (เผ็ด), เ precedes the initial consonant, ็ is above the initial consonant.

    2.  no tone mark.

    3.  อ , ิ , เ may or may not be followed by a final consonant.

        ็ must be followed by a final consonant.

บ may be the final consonant of ชอ or the first initial consonant of กิ (in case of two initial consonants).

4. ชอ-บกิน-เผ็ด makes no sense but ชอบ-กิน-เผ็ด means 'like to eat spicy (food)'.

5. no ́ sign.

**Example C:** วันนี้วันศุกร์ที่ 12 (*Today is Friday the 12th.*)

1. ̆ (วัน) is always above the initial consonant and followed by a final consonant.

2. ̂ (นี้) is always above the initial consonant and may or may not be followed by a final consonant.
   ́ comes above the initial consonant.

3. ̆ (วัน) is always above the initial consonant and followed by a final consonant.

4. ฺ (ศุกร์) is always underneath the initial consonant and may or may not be followed by a final consonant.
   ́ (ศุกร์) sign usually indicates the end of a word.

5. ̂ (ที่) is always above the initial consonant and may or may not be followed by a final consonant.
   ' comes above the initial consonant.

## COMPREHENSION EXERCISES

**A. Break the following sentences into individual words & read aloud.**

1. ฉันไม่รู้ — *I don't know.*
2. สีไม่สวย — *The color is not beautiful.*
3. เต็มแล้ว — *It's already full.*
4. ถูกและดี — *Cheap and good.*
5. จอดรถในบ้าน — *Park the car in the house.*
6. พี่ชายคุณ — *Your older brother.*
7. ลูกสาวผมชื่อเล็ก — *My daughter's name is Lek.*
8. คุณพ่อไม่ดื่มเบียร์ — *My father does not drink beer.*
9. อ่านได้แต่เขียนไม่ได้ — *Can read but cannot write.*
10. คุณแดงจะไปหาหมอ — *Daeng is going to see the doctor.*
11. คุณจะไปกี่โมง? — *What time will you go?*
12. เลี้ยวซ้าย ที่สี่แยก — *Turn left at the intersection.*

**B. Break the following text into individual words and read aloud.**

ตอนผมเป็นเด็กผมชอบเรียนภาษาจีนมากที่สุด แต่เพื่อนหลายคน
ไม่ชอบภาษานี้ บางคนบอกว่าภาษาจีนยากมาก บางคนบอกว่า ชอบภาษาอื่น
แล้วคุณล่ะ ชอบภาษาอะไรมากที่สุด?

*When I was young, I liked studying Chinese language the best. But many friends of mine did not like this language. Some said the language was very difficult, some said they liked other languages. What about you? What language do you like the best?*

**C. From the text above, find the Thai equivalents of the following words and write them down.**

1. to study      เรี _ _

2. friend      เพื่ _ _

3. many      ห _ _ _

4. difficult      ย _ _

5. language      ภ _ _ _

6. to like      _ _ _

7. some      _ _ ง

8. what?      อ _ _ _

9. but      แ _

10. not      _ _

11. very / a lot      _ _ _

12. to say / to tell      _ _ _

# LESSON 9: IRREGULAR PHONETICS

1. The vowel 'เ_' is usually pronounced short when there is a tone mark over the initial consonant, followed by a final consonant:

เก่ง        *skillful*        เล่น        *to play*

2. The vowel 'แ_' is usually pronounced short when there is tone mark '่' over the initial consonant, followed by a final consonant:

แน่น        *tight*        แว่นตา        *eye-glasses*

3. The vowel ' _อ_ ' , when combined with the following patterns, is usually pronounced short:

A. Any initial consonant + ' ่ ' + 'ง' or 'ย'

กล่อง        *box*        บ่อย        *often*

B. Initial Consonant Class 1 or 2 + ' ้ ' + either 'ง' or 'ย'

อ้อย        *sugar cane*        ห้อง        *room*

4. The vowels 'ไ_' and 'ใ_' can be pronounced <u>short</u> or <u>long</u> when there is a tone mark over the initial consonant. No rule applies. One can only learn these words by memorization.

ได้        <u>long</u>        *to get*

ไม้        <u>long</u>        *wood*

| ไม่ | short | *not* |
| เไล่ | short | *to expel* |
| เท้า | long | *foot* |
| เปล่า | long | *empty* |
| เก่า | short | *old* |
| เช่า | short | *to rent* |

# LESSON 10: Two Initial Consonants

Some Thai words have two initial consonants. The sound of the first initial consonant may be pronounced or may be silent, depending on the combination. We have seen some of the Two Initial Consonants in Lesson 6 where '**ห**' is used as a silent consonant before consonants Class 4 to produce certain tones and in Lesson 7 where '**อ**' is used as a silent consonant before consonant '**ย**'. This lesson will present more combinations of Two Initial Consonants.

When there is more than one initial consonant, the position of the vowel(s)[13] that come 'above' or 'below' the initial consonants is always attached to the last initial consonant. Observe the position of the vowels in these two examples:

| หนี | *to flee* | หนู | *mouse, rat* |
|-----|-----------|-----|--------------|

The position of the 'front' vowel(s) [13] is before the first initial consonant while the 'back' vowel(s) [13] come(s) after the second initial consonant. Observe the position of the vowels in these two examples:

| แหวน | *a ring* | หวาน | *sweet* |
|------|----------|------|---------|

The position of a tone mark is always above the second initial consonant or above the 'upper' vowel, if any. Examples:

| หน้า | *face, page* | หนี้ | *debt* |
|------|--------------|------|--------|
| แกล้ง | *to tease, pretend* | กล่อง | *a box* |

---

13. *Vowels can be in front of, behind, on top or below the initial consonant(s). See Lesson 3 for more details.*

There are several ways of reading a word with two initial consonants. Some are pronounced as a cluster, some have an inherent sound in between, and some combinations change to a new sound altogether. Details of these groups are as follows: ● **(12)**

**A) Two initial consonants which are pronounced together as a cluster usually have consonants 'ร' or 'ล' or 'ว' as their second consonant. The tone of a word is generally determined by the class of the first initial consonant.**

1. Examples of combinations with '**ก**':

| | | | |
|---|---|---|---|
| กรุง | *big city* | โกรธ | *angry* |
| กระโปรง | *skirt* | กรอบ | *crispy* |
| กลางคืน | *night time* | กลางวัน | *day time* |
| กลับ | *to return* | กลืน | *to swallow* |
| กล่อง | *box* | กล้วย | *banana* |
| กลม | *round* | ใกล้ | *near* |
| ไกล | *far* | กว่า | *more* |
| กว้าง | *wide* | กวาด | *to broom* |

2. Examples of combinations with '**ข**':

| | | | |
|---|---|---|---|
| ขรุขระ | *rough* | ขลาด | *coward* |
| ขลุ่ย | *flute* | ขวา | *right (direction)* |

3. Examples of combinations with '**ค**':

| | | | |
|---|---|---|---|
| ครับ | *particle* | ครู | *teacher* |

| | | | |
|---|---|---|---|
| ครัว | *kitchen* | เครียด | *stressed out* |
| เครื่องบิน | *plane* | ครอบครัว | *family* |
| คล้าย | *similar* | คลอง | *canal* |
| คลื่น | *wave* | ควัน | *smoke* |

4. Examples of combinations with '**ต**':

| | | | |
|---|---|---|---|
| ตรวจ | *to examine* | ตรง | *straight* |

5. Examples of combinations with '**ป**':

| | | | |
|---|---|---|---|
| ปรับ | *to adjust* | แปรง | *brush* |
| เปรี้ยว | *sour* | ประเทศ | *country* |
| แปล | *to translate* | ปลุก | *to wake up someone* |
| ปลา | *fish* | แปลก | *strange* |

6. Examples of combinations with '**พ**':

| | | | |
|---|---|---|---|
| เพราะ | *beautiful (sound)* | พระ | *monk* |
| พริก | *chili* | เพลง | *song* |

7. Examples of combinations with '**ผ**':

| | | | |
|---|---|---|---|
| ผลิต | *to produce* | ผลัด | *to take turns* |

**B) Some of the two initial consonant words are pronounced with inherent '_ะ' sound in between. The tone of a word is generally determined by the class of the first initial consonant.**

| Word | Pronunciation | Meaning |
|---|---|---|
| ขนาน | ขะ-หนาน | *parallel* |

| | | |
|---|---|---|
| ขนม | ขะ-หนม | *snack* |
| ถล่ม | ถะ-หล่ม | *to collapse* |
| ถนน | ถะ-หนน | *road* |
| ตลก | ตะ-หลก | *funny* |

However, when the first initial consonant is a member of Class 2 and the second initial consonant is a member of Class 3, the tones are applied according to their own classes.

| Word | Pronunciation | Meaning |
|---|---|---|
| สภาพ | สะ-พาบ | *condition* |
| สลัม | สะ-ลัม | *slum* |

When two syllables are put together as a compound word, the inherent ' ะ' usually appears after the first syllable.

| Word | Pronunciation | Meaning |
|---|---|---|
| ผลไม้ | ผน-ละ-ไม้ | *fruit* |
| คุณภาพ | คุน-นะ-พาบ | *quality* |

**C) Words that have a combination of two initial consonants and the vowels: 'เ_อ' , 'แ_' , 'เ_' , 'ไ_' , 'โ_' are read with inherent ' ะ' sound after the first initial consonant.**

| Word | Pronunciation | Meaning |
|---|---|---|
| เสมอ | สะ-เหมอ | *always* |
| แสดง | สะ-แดง | *to act* |
| แมลง | มะ-แลง | *insect* |

| เมล็ด | มะ-เล็ด | seed |
| ไถล | ถะ-ไหล | to wander off |
| โฉนด | ฉะ-โหนด | land deed |

## D) Some of the two initial consonant combinations are pronounced totally different than its original sounds.

'ทร' is pronounced as 'ซ' [14]

'ศร'/ 'สร' is pronounced as 'ส' [14]

| **Word** | **Pronunciation** | **Meaning** |
|---|---|---|
| ทราบ | ซาบ | to know |
| ทราย | ซาย | sand |
| ศรัทธา | สัด-ทา | faith |
| สร้าง | ส้าง | to build |
| เสร็จ | เส็ด | finished, done |

The only combination of 'จร' that is pronounced as 'จ' is:

| จริง | จิง | true |

## COMPREHENSION EXERCISES

## A. Which two initial consonants are pronounced as a cluster?

1. a) ตลอด   *throughout*     b) แกล้ง   *to tease*

2. a) แปลก   *strange*     b) สนุก   *fun*

3. a) กลุ่ม   *group*     b) ตลาด   *market*

4. a) พลาด   *to miss*     b) พร   *blessing*

---

*14. See rules of ' ร ' in Lesson 12.*

5. a) ผล     *classifier for fruits*    b) พร้อม     *ready*

## B. Read the following words.

| | | | |
|---|---|---|---|
| 1. จมูก | *nose* | 2. ตลาด | *market* |
| 3. ปล่อย | *to release* | 4. อร่อย | *delicious* |
| 5. ขนาด | *size* | 6. ขยัน | *diligent* |
| 7. สนุก | *fun* | 8. สนาม | *field* |
| 9. ฉลอง | *to celebrate* | 10. ถนน | *road* |
| 11. แพนง | *a Thai curry* | 12. แถลง | *to announce* |
| 13. เผด็จการ | *dictatorship* | 14. เสลด | *phlegm* |
| 15. โสร่ง | *sarong* | 16. เสนอ | *to propose* |
| 17. แผนก | *section* | 18. เจริญ | *to prosper* |
| 19. ฉลาม | *shark* | 20. เขมร | *Cambodia* |

# LESSON 11: PRONUNCIATION IRREGULARITIES

We have learnt the tone rules in the preceding lessons. However, there are some exceptions to the rules. This lesson presents important irregularities in pronunciation.

1. There are some disyllabic words that were transformed from monosyllabic words. After transformation, the tone of the second syllable is usually determined by the consonant class of the first syllable.

   **Examples:**

   | Word | Pronunciation | Meaning |
   |------|---------------|---------|
   | ตำรวจ (from ตรวจ) | ตำ-หรวด | *police* |
   | สำเร็จ (from เสร็จ) | สำ-เหร็ด | *successful* |
   | สำรวจ (from สรวจ) | สำ-หรวด | *to survey* |

2. In some polysyllabic words, the tone of the second or the third syllable is determined by the class of the preceding initial consonant. There is no clear explanation for this but frequently used words are listed below:

   **Examples:**

   | Word | Pronunciation | Meaning |
   |------|---------------|---------|
   | ประโยชน์ | ประ-โหยด | *useful* |
   | ประวัติ | ประ-หวัด | *record, history* |
   | ศักราช | สัก-กะ-หราด | *an era* |
   | วาสนา | วาด-สะ-หนา | *fortune* |
   | ริษยา | ริด-สะ-หยา | *jealousy* |

3. Some compound words are pronounced a little different from the same words in isolation.

**Examples**:

ขอโทษ *(to apologize)* is a combination of ขอ and โทษ but when put together, the sound of ขอ is slightly shortened.

น้ำปลา *(fish sauce)* is a combination of น้ำ and ปลา but when put together, the sound of น้ำ is slightly shortened.

# LESSON 12: Rules of '  ร  '

The consonant 'ร' plays a special role in the Thai language. Depending on its combination with other consonants and vowels, its pronunciation can change. This lesson lists the most important deviations from the rules we discussed earlier.

1. 'ร' as a final consonant is read 'น' when preceded by a written vowel (as opposed to an omitted vowel).

   **Examples:**

   | Word | Pronunciation | Meaning |
   |------|--------------|---------|
   | อาหาร | อา-หาน | *food* |
   | สงสาร | สง-สาน | *to pity* |
   | สมควร | สม-ควน | *to deserve* |
   | ทหาร | ทะ-หาน | *soldier* |
   | ธนาคาร | ทะ-นา-คาน | *bank* |

2. When appearing after an initial consonant without a written vowel, 'ร' is read '-อน'.

   **Examples:**

   | Word | Pronunciation | Meaning |
   |------|--------------|---------|
   | ละคร | ละ-คอน | *a play* |
   | อักษร | อัก-สอน | *an alphabet* |

3. When appearing in the middle of a polysyllabic word, 'ร' is usually read '-ระ'.

**Examples:**

| Word | Pronunciation | Meaning |
|------|---------------|---------|
| สารสิน | สา-ระ-สิน | *a road's name* |
| บารมี | บา-ระ-มี | *charisma* |
| วารสาร | วา-ระ-สาน | *a journal* |
| สารภาพ | สา-ระ-พาบ | *to confess* |

A frequently seen word that does not follow this rule, but is pronounced 'น' instead of 'ระ' is

| Word | Pronunciation | Meaning |
|------|---------------|---------|
| มารดา | มาน-ดา | *mother* |

4. In a polysyllabic word, when 'ร' is placed immediately behind the initial consonant, without any vowels attached to the initial consonant, and followed by another syllable, the inherent '_อ' is usually pronounced between the two initial consonants.

**Examples:**

| Word | Pronunciation | Meaning |
|------|---------------|---------|
| บริษัท | บอ-ริ-สัด | *company* |
| มรดก | มอ-ระ-ดก | *inheritance* |
| จระเข้ | จอ-ระ-เข้ | *crocodile* |
| ทรยศ | ทอ-ระ-ยด | *to betray* |
| กรณี | กอ-ระ-นี | *a case* |
| ทรมาน | ทอ-ระ-มาน | *to suffer* |

5. When used as the second initial consonant in a two initial consonant combination preceded by 'ศ' or 'ส' as the first consonant, 'ร' is usually silent.

**Examples:**

| Word | Pronunciation | Meaning |
|------|--------------|---------|
| เศร้า | เส้า | *sad* |
| ศรัทธา | สัด-ทา | *faith* |
| ศรีลังกา | สี-ลัง-กา | *Sri Lanka* |
| สร้อย | ส้อย | *necklace* |
| สร้าง | ส้าง | *to build* |
| เสร็จ | เส็ด | *finished* |
| สระ | สะ | *pool* |

6. In monosyllabic words (except some loan words), when used as the second initial consonant in a two initial consonant combination preceded by 'ท ' as the first consonant, 'ทร' is pronounced 'ซ'.

**Examples:**

| Word | Pronunciation | Meaning |
|------|--------------|---------|
| ทราบ | ซาบ | *to know* |
| ทรงผม | ซง-ผม | *hair style* |
| ทราย | ซาย | *sand* |

This rule does not apply to some loan words. The example below shows that the two consonants are pronounced together as a cluster.

| | | |
|------|--------------|---------|
| แทร็กเตอร์ | แทร็ก-เตอ | *tractor* |

7. Double 'ร' or 'รร' (raw hăhn), is used to write some of the Sanskrit and Khmer words. When no final consonant follows, 'รร' is read ' ั น', when it comes just after an initial consonant and is followed by a final consonant, 'รร' is read ' ั '.

**Examples:**

| Word | Pronunciation | Meaning |
|---|---|---|
| บรรเทา | บัน-เทา | *to relieve* |
| กรรไกร | กัน-ไก | *scissors* |
| พรรค | พัค | *political party* |
| ธรรมดา | ทัม-มะ-ดา | *normal* |
| กรรมการ | กัม-มะ-กาน | *committee* |

## COMPREHENSION EXERCISES

**A. Space the words apart and read the sentences aloud.**

1. เราจะสร้างที่ทำงานใหม่

   *We are going to build a new office.*

2. เราทำงานเสร็จแล้ว

   *We have finished our work.*

3. หาดทรายที่นี่สวยมาก

   *The beach here is very beautiful.*

4. ธรรมดาทหารชอบมาที่นี่

   *Normally the soldiers like to come here.*

5. ไม่ทราบค่ะ

   *I don't know.*

## B. Find out the tones of the following words and pronounce them aloud.

1. สร้าง      2. เสร็จ      3. ทราย

4. พรรค      5. ทราบ      6. เศร้า

# LESSON 13: Miscellaneous Signs

The Thai written language makes use of a variety of signs, which affect the pronunciation of the words. This lesson presents the most frequently used signs, and explains their functions.

1. ๆ (ไม้ยมก), pronounced 'mái yah-móhk', always placed behind a word, indicates that the preceding word is to be voiced twice.

   **Example:**

   | Word | Pronunciation | Meaning |
   |------|---------------|---------|
   | พูดดังๆ | พูด-ดัง-ดัง | *speak louder* |

2. ์ (การันต์), pronounced 'gah-rahn', always placed above a consonant, indicates that the consonant below is silent.

   **Example:**

   | Word | Pronunciation | Meaning |
   |------|---------------|---------|
   | สัตว์ | สัด | *animal* |

3. ฯ (ไปยาลน้อย), pronounced 'bpai-yahn-nói', always placed behind a word, indicates that a proper name has been abbreviated.

   **Example:**

   | Word | Proper name | Meaning |
   |------|-------------|---------|
   | กรุงเทพฯ | กรุงเทพมหานคร | *Bangkok* |

4. ฯลฯ (ไปยาลใหญ่), pronounced 'bpai-yahn-yài', always placed behind a word, is equivalent to 'etc.' in English.

**Example:**

| Word | Meaning |
|---|---|
| รถ รถไฟ เครื่องบิน ฯลฯ | *car, train, plane, etc.* |

5. ็ (ไม้ไต่คู้), pronounced 'mái-dtài-kóo', always placed above the initial consonant, shortens the vowels 'เ_' and 'แ_ _'.

**Examples:**

| Word | Composition | Meaning |
|---|---|---|
| แข็ง | ข + แ-ะ + ง | *hard* |
| เล็ง | ล + เ-ะ + ง | *to aim* |

# LESSON 14: Silent Vowels & Consonants

1. When vowels ' ◌ุ ' or ' ◌ิ ' are combined with certain consonants at the end of a word, the vowels are not pronounced. These combination include: 'ตุ', 'ติ', 'ดิ' , 'มิ'

   **Examples:**

   | Word | Pronunciation | Meaning |
   |------|---------------|---------|
   | เหตุการณ์ | เหด-กาน | *incident* |
   | เหตุผล | เหด-ผน | *reason* |
   | สาเหตุ | สา-เหด | *cause* |
   | ชาติ | ชาด | *nation* |
   | ญาติ | ยาด | *relatives* |
   | ประวัติ | ประ-หวัด | *background* |
   | สมมุติ | สม-มุด | *to suppose* |
   | จักรพรรดิ | จัก-กระ-พัด | *emperor* |
   | ภูมิใจ | พูม-ใจ | *to be proud* |

2. Silent consonants are not always marked with ' ◌์ ' as mentioned in Lesson 13: Miscellaneous Signs. 'ร', when appearing after a Stop Final Consonant[15] is often not pronounced.

   **Examples:**

   | Word | Pronunciation | Meaning |
   |------|---------------|---------|
   | สมัคร | สะ-หมัก | *to apply* |

---

15. *See Lesson 5 for the classification of Final Consonants.*

| | | |
|---|---|---|
| บัตร | บัด | *card* |
| เกษตร | กะ-เสด | *agriculture* |

3. 'ร' and 'ห', when appearing in the middle of some words are not pronounced.

**Examples:**

| Word | Pronunciation | Meaning |
|---|---|---|
| สามารถ | สา-สาด | *to be able to* |
| เกียรติ | เกียด | *honor* |
| พราหมณ์ | พราม | *Brahman* |

4. Some words have more than one or two final consonants. The last final consonant may appear with the silence sign. In this case, only pronounce the first final consonant.

**Examples:**

| Word | Pronunciation | Meaning |
|---|---|---|
| ดวงจันทร์ | ดวง-จัน | *moon* |
| ภาพลักษณ์ | พาบ-ลัก | *image* |

## COMPREHENSION EXERCISE

**A. Break the text below into individual words and write down the words that have silent consonants as well as their equivalent meaning in English.**

ญาติผมไม่สามารถไปสมัครงานที่กระทรวงเกษตรได้เพราะว่าเป็น ชาวต่าง ชาติ

| Thai | English |
|------|---------|
| 1. _____ | _____ |
| 2. _____ | _____ |
| 3. _____ | _____ |
| 4. _____ | _____ |
| 5. _____ | _____ |

# LESSON 15: About ' ฤ '

'ฤ' represents a combination of a consonant and a vowel sound. It has three different pronunciations. There are not many words spelt with 'ฤ'. The words that you may come across occasionally are as follows.

1.  Having the 'เรอ' sound.
    **Example:**

    | Word | Pronunciation | Meaning |
    |------|---------------|---------|
    | ฤกษ์ | เริก | *auspicious* |

2.  Having the 'ริ' sound.
    **Examples:**

    | Word | Pronunciation | Meaning |
    |------|---------------|---------|
    | อังกฤษ | อัง-กริด | *England* |
    | ทฤษฎี | ทริด-สะ-ดี | *theory* |
    | ฤทธิ์ | ริด | *effect, power* |

3.  Having the 'รี' sound.
    **Example:**

    | Word | Pronunciation | Meaning |
    |------|---------------|---------|
    | ฤดู | รี-ดู | *season* |

When preceded by 'พ', the two sounds are pronounced together.

**Examples:**

| Word | Pronunciation | Meaning |
|------|---------------|---------|
| พฤษภาคม | พรึด- สะ- พา- คม | *May* |
| พฤศจิกายน | พรึด-สะ-จิ-กา-ยน | *November* |
| พฤหัสบดี | พรี-หัด-สะ-บอ-ดี | *Thursday* |
| พฤติกรรม | พรึด-ติ-กัม | *Behavior* |

# LESSON 16: Unusual Spellings

This lesson presents the two most common words that have unusual spellings.

1. 'ก็', pronounced 'ก้อ', is used widely and regularly among Thais, especially when speaking. This word has several meanings and functions. It is widely used in conditional sentences and on some occasions, it means 'also'.

   **Examples:**

   อันนี้ก็สวย อันนั้นก็ดี
   *This one is also beautiful,*
   *that one is also good.*

   ถ้าคุณไปผมก็ไป
   *If you go, I will go too.*

2. 'ณ', pronounced 'นะ', means 'at' or 'in' (a preposition used to indicate location). It is only used in a formal context.

   **Example:**

   ณ กรุงลอนดอน
   *in London*

# LESSON 17: Twenty ' ไ ' Thai Words

There are only 20 words in Thai that are spelled with the vowel 'ไ_'. All other words with the vowel sound 'ai' are either spelled with 'ไ_' or '_ัย'. The 16 most commonly used words containing the vowel 'ไ_' are:

|  |  |
|------|---------|
| ใจ | mind, heart |
| ให้ | to give |
| ใน | in |
| ใหม่ | new |
| ใส | clear, transparent |
| ใคร | who |
| ใช้ | to use |
| ใส่ | to put in, to put on |
| ใต้ | under |
| ใหญ่ | big |
| ใกล้ | near |
| ใช่ | yes, right |
| ใบ | leaf |
| สะใภ้ | in law (female) |
| ใบ้ | dumb |
| หลงใหล | to be enchanted |

The following 4 words are not frequently used:

|  |  |
|------|---------|
| ใคร่ | to desire |
| ใย | fiber, web |

ใฝ่             *to have an interest in*

ใด             *which?*

## COMPREHENSION EXERCISE

**A. Complete the sentences below and read them aloud.**

1. คนที่พูดไม่ได้เรียกว่าคน _____

 *A person who can't speak is called _____.*

2. รองเท้าอยู่ _____ ตู้รองเท้า

 *The shoes are \_\_\_\_\_ the shoe closet.*

3. แมวนอนอยู่_____โต๊ะ

 *A cat is lying _____ the table.*

4. บ้านหลังนี้ _____ มาก

 *This house is very _____.*

5. ผมไม่ _____ คนออสเตรเลีย

 *I am not Australian.*

6. ต้นไม้ต้นนั้นมี _____ สีแดง

 *That tree has red \_\_\_\_\_ .*

7. โปรแกรมนี้ _____ ยังไง?

 *How do you _____ this program?*

8. คุณแม่_____ หนังสือคุณพ่อ

   *My mother _____ my father a book.*

9. _____ อยู่ที่นั่น?

   *_____ is there?*

10. บ้านฉันอยู่ _____ ตลาด

    *My house is _____ the market.*

11. น้ำทะเล _____มาก

    *The sea water is very _____.*

12. เพื่อนคุณเป็นคน _____ ดี

    *Your friend is a good _____ person.*

# LESSON 18: Words of Similar Pronunciation

The following pairs of words have the same initial consonant sound. Some paired words differ in their tones, vowels, or both. These subtle differences often cause a lot of confusion and misunderstanding among foreigners. Observe the meaning and read them aloud.

| | | |
|---|---|---|
| ทุก | high tone | *every* |
| ถูก | low tone | *cheap, correct* |
| | | |
| หาย | rising tone | *missing* |
| ให้ | falling tone | *to give, for* |
| | | |
| สูง | rising tone | *tall* |
| ซุง | mid tone | *log* |
| | | |
| แหวน | rising tone | *ring* |
| แว่น | falling tone | *glasses* |
| | | |
| บ่น | low tone | *to complain* |
| บน | mid tone | *on* |
| | | |
| ช่าง | falling tone | *mechanic* |
| ช้าง | high tone | *elephant* |

| ยุง | mid tone | *mosquito* |
|-----|----------|------------|
| ยุ่ง | falling tone | *busy* |
| สด | low tone | *fresh* |
| โสด | low tone | *single* |
| ขาด | low tone | *lack* |
| คาด | falling tone | *to anticipate* |
| ขอ | rising tone | *to request* |
| คอ | mid tone | *throat* |
| หย่า | low tone | *to divorce* |
| อย่า | low tone | *Don't!* |
| หวาน | rising tone | *sweet* |
| วัน | mid tone | *day* |
| ส้ม | falling tone | *orange* |
| ซ่อม | falling tone | *to fix* |
| ฝัน | rising tone | *to dream* |
| ฟัน | mid tone | *teeth* |
| ใหม่ | low tone | *new* |
| ไม่ | falling tone | *not* |

| | | |
|---|---|---|
| ลง | mid tone | *down* |
| ลอง | mid tone | *to try* |
| | | |
| หลัง | rising tone | *behind* |
| ล่าง | falling tone | *below* |
| | | |
| ร้าน | high tone | *shop* |
| ร้อน | high tone | *hot* |
| | | |
| อยาก | low tone | *to want to* |
| ยาก | falling tone | *difficult* |

The following pairs of words have similar initial consonant sounds. Some paired words are different in their tones, vowels, or both. Observe the meaning and read them aloud.

| | | |
|---|---|---|
| เก่า | low tone | *old* |
| เข่า | low tone | *knee* |
| | | |
| กับ | low tone | *with, and* |
| ขับ | low tone | *to drive* |
| | | |
| เพื่อน | falling tone | *friend* |
| เปื้อน | falling tone | *to stain* |
| | | |
| หนึ่ง | low tone | *one* |
| เงิน | mid tone | *money* |

| | | |
|---|---|---|
| เดือน | mid tone | *month* |
| เตือน | mid tone | *to warn, remind* |

The following pairs of words sound exactly the same but differ in their spelling.

| | | |
|---|---|---|
| รส | high tone | *flavor* |
| รถ | high tone | *car* |
| | | |
| รัด | high tone | *to tighten* |
| รัฐ | high tone | *state, territory* |
| | | |
| ค่า | falling tone | *value, price* |
| ฆ่า | falling tone | *to kill* |
| | | |
| สุก | low tone | *ripe, cooked* |
| สุข | low tone | *happy* |

## COMPREHENSION EXERCISE

**A. Select the correct missing words.**

1. _____ ไปที่นั่น   *Don't go there!*

   a) อย่า            b) หย่า

2. _____ น้ำสองขวดครับ   *May I have two bottles of water please?*

   a) คอ            b) ขอ

3. _____ กินอาหารเผ็ด   *I want to eat spicy food.*
   a) อยาก          b) ยาก

4. วันนี้ผม _____ มาก   *I am very busy today.*
   a) ยุง          b) ยุ่ง

5. _____จอดรถเท่าไรคะ?   *How much is the parking fee?*
   a) ฆ่า          b) ค่า

6. ที่ประเทศไทยของ _____   *Things are inexpensive in Thailand.*
   a) ทุก          b) ถูก

7. ห้องน้ำอยู่ชั้น_____ค่ะ   *The toilet is downstairs.*
   a) ล่าง          b) หลัง

# LESSON 19: Main Vocabulary lists

## Vocabulary list by order of consonants

| | | | | |
|---|---|---|---|---|
| ก | ไก่ | กับ | กิน | เก็บ |
| | chicken | with | to eat | to keep |
| | กด | แกง | กลับ | |
| | to press | curry | to return | |

| | | | | |
|---|---|---|---|---|
| ข | ไข่ | ขวด | ขาย | ของ |
| | egg | bottle | to sell | things |
| | ขม | ขาว | | |
| | bitter | white | | |

| | | | | |
|---|---|---|---|---|
| ค | ควาย | คน | เคย | คิด |
| | buffalo | person | used to | to think |
| | คอย | เค็ม | | |
| | to wait | salty | | |

| | | | |
|---|---|---|---|
| ฆ | ระฆัง | ฆ่า | ฆ้อง |
| | big bell | to kill | gong |

| | | | | |
|---|---|---|---|---|
| ง | งู | งอน | ง่วง | งง |
| | snake | petulant | sleepy | confused |
| | ง่าย | งาน | เงิน | |
| | easy | job | money | |

| | | | | |
|---|---|---|---|---|
| จ | จาน | จอง | จืด | จด |
| | *plate* | *to reserve* | *bland taste* | *to note* |
| | จอด | จน | เจอ | |
| | *to park* | *poor* | *to meet* | |
| | | | | |
| ฉ | ฉิ่ง | ฉีก | ฉบับ | ฉลอง |
| | *cymbals* | *to tear* | *classifier* | *to celebrate* |
| | | | *for magazine* | |
| | ฉลาด | ฉัน | | |
| | *smart* | *I, me* | | |
| | | | | |
| ช | ช้าง | ชอบ | ชน | ชาว |
| | *elephant* | *to like* | *to bump* | *people, tribe* |
| | ชาติ | ชม | | |
| | *nation* | *to praise* | | |
| | | | | |
| ซ | โซ่ | ซอย | ซอง | ซ้ำ |
| | *chain* | *soi* | *envelop* | *repeatedly* |
| | ซื้อ | ซ่อม | | |
| | *to buy* | *to fix* | | |
| | | | | |
| ฌ | เฌอ | | | |
| | *a kind of tree* | | | |
| | | | | |
| ญ | หญิง | หญ้า | ใหญ่ | |
| | *woman, girl* | *grass* | *big* | |

ฎ    ชฎา      กรกฎาคม
     *Head-dress*    *July*

ฏ    ปฏัก      ปฏิทิน      ปฏิบัติ      ปฏิเสธ
     *goad*      *calendar*      *to carry out*      *to refuse*

ฐ    ฐาน      ฐานะ
     *base*      *position, status*

ฑ    มณโฑ
     *a female character in Ramayana* [16]

ฒ    ผู้เฒ่า      พัฒนา      วัฒนธรรม
     *old man*      *to develop*      *culture*

ณ    เณร      ลักษณะ
     *novice*      *characteristic*

ด    เด็ก      ดึก      เดือน      ดำ
     *child*      *late at night*      *month*      *black*
     ดู      ด้วย      ดัง
     *to watch*      *also*      *loud*

ต    เต่า      ตอน      ตื่น      ตัว
     *turtle*      *at, when*      *to wake up*      *body*

16. *Ramayana is a Thai epic influenced by the Ramayana of India.*

|   | ต้อง | ตาย | ต้น | ตอบ |
|---|---|---|---|---|
|   | *must* | *to die* | *blocked* | *to answer* |
| ถ | ถุง | ถอน | แถว | ถ้า |
|   | *bag* | *to withdraw* | *row, line* | *if* |
|   | ถือ | ถู | ถาม |   |
|   | *to carry* | *to mob* | *to ask a question* |   |
| ท | ทหาร | ทาน | เที่ยว | ทำ |
|   | *soldier* | *to eat* | *to travel* | *to do, make* |
|   | ทุก | ที่ | ทอด | ไทย |
|   | *every* | *at* | *to deep fry* | *Thai* |
| ธ | ธง | ธนาคาร | ธรรม | ธันวาคม |
|   | *flag* | *bank* | *Dharma* | *December* |
|   | ธุระ | ธุรกิจ |   |   |
|   | *errand* | *business* |   |   |
| น | หนู | นาน | นอน | นอก |
|   | *rat* | *long* | *to sleep* | *outside* |
|   | ใน | นี่ | นัด |   |
|   | *in* | *this* | *appointment* |   |
| บ | ใบไม้ | บ้าน | บ้า | บอก |
|   | *leaf* | *house* | *crazy* | *to tell* |

เบา
*light* (*not heavy*)

เบื่อ
*bored*

ป | ปลา | ปาก | แปด | ปิด
--- | --- | --- | --- | ---
| *fish* | *mouth* | *eight* | *to close, to turn off*
| เปียก | ป่วย | เปิด |
| *wet* | *sick* | *to open, to turn on* |

ผ | ผึ้ง | ผ้า | ผิด | ผูก
--- | --- | --- | --- | ---
| *bee* | *cloth* | *wrong* | *to tie*
| แผล | ผล | ผู้หญิง | ผู้ชาย
| *wound* | *result* | *female* | *male*

ฝ | ฝา | ฝน | ฝัน | ฝรั่ง
--- | --- | --- | --- | ---
| *lid* | *rain* | *dream* | *guava, Caucasian*
| ฝาก | ฝุ่น | |
| *to entrust* | *dust* | |

พ | พาน | พูด | เพื่อน | พบ
--- | --- | --- | --- | ---
| *chalice* | *to speak* | *friend* | *to meet*
| พวก | แพ้ | |
| *group* | *allergic* | |

ฟ | ฟัน | ฟอง | ฟ้า | ฟรี
--- | --- | --- | --- | ---
| *tooth* | *bubble* | *light blue* | *cost nothing*

|  | ฟัง | แฟน |  |  |
|---|---|---|---|---|
|  | to listen, | girlfriend, boyfriend |  |  |
| ภ | สำเภา | ภรรยา | ภัตตาคาร | ภัย |
|  | ship | wife | restaurant | danger |
|  | ภาค | ภาพ | ภาษา |  |
|  | region | picture | language |  |
| ม | ม้า | มี | มา | มาก |
|  | house | to have to | come | a lot |
|  | เมื่อ | หมอ | เมือง |  |
|  | when (conj.) | doctor | city, country |  |
| ย | ยักษ์ | ยา | ยาก | ยอม |
|  | giant | medicine | difficult | to consent |
|  | แยก | ยุ่ง |  |  |
|  | to separate | busy |  |  |
| ร | เรือ | รัก | เรียก | รีบ |
|  | boat | to love | to call | to hurry |
|  | รู้ | เรื่อง | รถ | รอ |
|  | to know | matter, story | vehicle | to wait |
| ล | ลิง | ล้าน | ลง | เลือก |
|  | monkey | million | to go down | to choose |

|   | | | |
|---|---|---|---|
| | ลอง | และ | ลับ | ลัด |
| | to try | and | secret | to take a short cut |
| ว | แหวน | วัน | วัด | แว่น |
| | ring | day | temple | glasses |
| | วงกลม | วัว | | |
| | circle | cow | | |
| ศ | ศาลา | ศัพท์ | ศอก | ลูกศิษย์ |
| | pavilion | vocabulary | elbow | student |
| | ศาล | เศร้า | | |
| | court | sad | | |
| ษ | ฤๅษี | การเกษตร | | |
| | hermit | agriculture | | |
| ส | เสือ | เสื้อ | สด | โสด |
| | tiger | shirt | fresh | single |
| | สี | สอน | สอง | สูบ |
| | color | to teach | two | to smoke |
| ห | หีบ | ห้า | หา | หู |
| | box | five | to look for | ear |
| | ห้อง | ให้ | ห้าม | หยุด |
| | room | to give | Don't! | stop |

| พ | จุฬา |
|---|------|
|   | *a Thai kite* |

| อ | อ่าง | อดทน | อบ | เอา |
|---|------|------|-----|-----|
|   | *tub, basin* | *to endure* | *to bake* | *to want something* |
|   | อ้วน | อาย | อะไร | อาบน้ำ |
|   | *fat* | *shy* | *what?* | *to bathe, to shower* |

| ฮ | นกฮูก |
|---|-------|
|   | *owl* |

## Extra vocabulary list by class of Initial Consonant

| Class 1 ก จ ด ต ฎ ฏ บ ป อ |
|---|

| ก | กัน | กาว | กี่ | เก่ง |
|---|-----|-----|-----|-----|
|   | *together* | *glue* | *how many?* | *skillful* |
|   | กุ้ง | กางเกง | แก่ | แก้ |
|   | *shrimp* | *trousers* | *old (person)* | *to fix* |
|   | โกง | เกาะ | กอง | ก่อน |
|   | *to cheat* | *island* | *pile* | *before, first* |
|   | เก่า | เกิน | เกือบ | กลับ |
|   | *old (thing)* | *to exceed* | *almost* | *to return* |
|   | กลัว | ไกล | ใกล้ | เก้า |
|   | *be afraid* | *far* | *near* | *nine* |

| จ | จะ | จัด | จาก | จุด |
|---|---|---|---|---|
| | will/shall | to arrange | from | dot |
| | เจ็บ | เจ็ด | แจก | จูง |
| | hurt | seven | to hand out | to lead (by hand) |
| | จบ | โจร | จ้อง | จำ |
| | to end | robber | to stare | to memorize |

| ด | ด้าน | ได้ | ดี | ดึง |
|---|---|---|---|---|
| | side | to get, be able | good | to pull |
| | ดื่ม | ดิบ | ดม | เดิน |
| | to drink | raw | to smell | to walk |
| | เดี๋ยว | ด่วน | โดน | |
| | hold on! | urgent | to bump against | |

| ต | ต้น | ตัด | ตา | ตาม |
|---|---|---|---|---|
| | clogged | to cut | eye | to follow |
| | ตู้ | ติด | ติดต่อ | เตือน |
| | cabinet | to stick | to contact | to remind, warn |
| | เตะ | เต็ม | เต้น | แตก |
| | to kick | full | to dance | shattered |
| | แตกต่าง | ตกแต่ง | โต๊ะ | โต |
| | different | to decorate | desk/table | big |
| | ตก | ต้ม | ตอบ | ตอน |
| | to fall | to boil | to answer | when (conj.) |
| | ต้อง | เติม | เตียง | เตี้ย |
| | must | to fill | bed | short |

ต่ำ      ใต้

*low*      *under, below*

| บ | บาง | บาท | บ้าง | บ่าย |
|---|---|---|---|---|
| | *some* | *baht* | *some, any* | *afternoon* |
| | บิน | บีบ | บุญ | บูด |
| | *to fly* | *to squeeze* | *merit* | *bad, spoiled* |
| | แบน | แบ่ง | บน | บ่น |
| | *flat* | *to divide* | *on* | *to complain* |
| | เบาะ | บอก | บอด | บวก |
| | *mattress* | *to tell* | *blind* | *plus* |
| | เบา | | ใบ | |
| | *light, not heavy* | | *classifier for leaves, plates, papers* | |

| ป | ปาก | ป่า | ป้า | ปี |
|---|---|---|---|---|
| | *mouth* | *forest* | *aunt* | *year* |
| | ปีก | ปีน | ปู | เป็น |
| | *wing* | *to climb* | *crab* | *to be* |
| | แป้ง | ปวด | ไป | เป่า |
| | *powder* | *ache* | *to go* | *to blow* |

| อ | อ่าน | อิ่ม | อีก | อุ่น |
|---|---|---|---|---|
| | *to read* | *full (stomach)* | *more, again* | *warm* |
| | อื่น | โอ่ง | อด | ออก |
| | *others* | *deep tub* | *to refrain from* | *out* |

| | | | |
|---|---|---|---|
| เอียง | อวด | ไอ | เอา |
| *to incline* | *to show off* | *to cough* | *to want* |

## Class 2 ข ฉ ถ ฐ ผ ฝ ส ศ ษ ห

**ข**

| | | | |
|---|---|---|---|
| ขับ | ขาด | ขา | ข่าว |
| *to drive* | *lack* | *leg* | *news* |
| ข้าม | ข้าง | ข้าว | ขิง |
| *to cross* | *side* | *rice* | *ginger* |
| ขีด | ขี้ | ขึ้น | เข็ม |
| *to draw a line* | *excrement* | *to go up* | *needle* |
| แข็ง | แขน | ขม | ขน |
| *hard* | *arm* | *bitter flavor* | *body hair* |
| ขอ | ขอบ | เขียน | เขิน |
| *to ask for* | *edge* | *to write* | *shy* |
| ขวด | ขวบ | ขำ | ไข่ |
| *bottle* | *year(classifier)* | *funny, laugh* | *egg* |
| ไข้ | เข้า | เข่า | |
| *fever* | *to enter* | *knee* | |

**ฉ**

| | | |
|---|---|---|
| ฉาย | ฉีด | เฉย |
| *to project,* | *to spray,* | *to stay calm,* |
| *to radiate* | *to inject* | *to do nothing* |

**ถ**

| | | | |
|---|---|---|---|
| ถึง | ถูก | เถอะ | ถ้ำ |
| *till* | *cheap, correct* | *urging particle* | *cave* |

| ถอน | ถอย | ถ้วย | แถม |
|------|------|------|------|
| to withdraw | to retreat | cup | to give away |
| ถัง | ถาม | | |
| bucket | to ask a question | | |

| ฐ | ฐานะ | | |
|------|------|------|------|
| | status | | |

| ผ | ผัด | ผัก | ผิว | แผ่น |
|------|------|------|------|------|
| | to stir fry | vegetable | skin | paper's classifier |
| | ผื่น | เผ็ด | ผม | ผล |
| | rash | spicy | hair, I (male) | result |
| | ผอม | เผื่อ | ผัว | |
| | thin | in case | husband | |

| ฝ | ฝ่าย | ฝืด | ฝน | เฝ้า |
|------|------|------|------|------|
| | side | unsmooth | rain | to guard |
| | ฝัง | ฝุ่น | | |
| | to bury | dust | | |

| ส | สับ | สั้น | สั่ง | สาม |
|------|------|------|------|------|
| | to chop | short | to order | three |
| | สาว | สาย | สิบ | สิ่ง |
| | young woman | late | ten | thing |
| | สุก | สี่ | สูง | แสน |
| | ripe | four | tall | hundred thousand |

| ส้อม | ส้ม | เสีย | เสือ |
|------|------|------|------|
| fork | orange | broken | tiger |
| เสื่อ | เสื้อ | สวด | สวม |
| mat | shirt | to chant | to wear |
| สวย | ใส | ใส่ | เสา |
| beautiful | transparent | to wear | pole |

ศ -

ษ -

| ห | หา | ห้าง | หาด | หาย |
|---|------|------|------|------|
| | to seek | shopping mall | beach | missing |
| | แห้ง | หิว | เห็น | หอม |
| | dry | hungry | to see | good smell |
| | ห่วง | หก | หวง | หอย |
| | to worry | six | possessive | shell |

**Class 3**   ค ฆ ช ฌ ฑ ฒ ฑ ฒ พ ภ ฟ ซ ฮ

| ค | คะ | คับ | คัน | ค่า |
|---|------|------|------|------|
| | final particle | tight | itchy | value, fee |
| | ค้า | คาง | คู่ | แค่ |
| | trade | chin | pair | only |
| | คือ | เค็ม | โค้ง | คืน |
| | to be | salty | curve | night (classifier) |

| คม | คน | คอย | เคย |
|----|----|-----|-----|
| *sharp* | *person* | *to wait* | *have ever* |
| คำ | เค้า | | |
| *word* | *he/she* | | |

ฅ  −

| ช | ช้า | ชาม | ชาย | ชิด |
|---|-----|-----|-----|-----|
| | *slow* | *bowl* | *male* | *to stay close to* |
| | ชิม | ชิ้น | ชุด | เช็ด |
| | *to taste* | *piece* | *a set of* | *to wipe* |
| | ชื่อ | เช้า | เชิญ | เชื่อ |
| | *name* | *morning* | *to invite* | *to believe* |
| | ช้อน | ช่อง | ช่วย | ใช่ |
| | *spoon* | *gap* | *to help* | *yes, right!* |
| | ใช้ | เช่า | | |
| | *to use* | *to rent* | | |

ฌ  −

| ท | ทา | ท่า | ทิศ | ทาง |
|---|-----|-----|-----|-----|
| | *to smear* | *posture* | *direction* | *way* |
| | ทาน | ท้าย | ที | เท |
| | *to eat* | *rear* | *time (classifier)* | *to pour* |

| | | | |
|---|---|---|---|
| ทอง | เที่ยง | เท้า | ทอน |
| gold | noon | feet | to change (money) |
| ทวน | ไทย | เทา | ทน |
| to review | Thai | gray | to endure |

| | | | |
|---|---|---|---|
| ธ | ธง | ฐูป | เธอ |
| | flag | incense stick | you, her |

ฑ   –

ฒ   พัฒนา
to develop

| | | | |
|---|---|---|---|
| พ | พัก | พัด | พัน | พา |
| | to rest | to blow | thousand | to bring (someone ) |
| | พี่ | แพง | เพียง | เพื่อ |
| | older sibling | expensive | only | for |
| | พอ | พวก | พูด | |
| | enough | group | speak | |

| | | |
|---|---|---|
| ภ | ภาค | ภาษา |
| | region | language |

| | | | |
|---|---|---|---|
| ฟ | ฟัง | ฟ้า | ไฟ | ไฟฟ้า |
| | to listen | sky | light, fire | electricity |

| ซ | ซ้าย | แซง | ซอง | ซัก |
|---|------|------|------|-----|
|   | *left* | *to overtake* | *envelop* | *to wash (clothes)* |
|   | ซ้ำ |  |  |  |
|   | *repeatedly* |  |  |  |

| ฮ | เฮง |
|---|-----|
|   | *good fortune* |

---

**Class 4    ง ย ญ น ณ  ร ล ฬ ว ม & ห in front of class 4**

---

| ง | งาม | งีบ | งอ | เงียบ |
|---|-----|-----|-----|-------|
|   | *beautiful* | *take a nap* | *bent* | *quiet* |
|   | เงิน | เงา |  |  |
|   | *money* | *shadow* |  |  |

| ย | ยัง | ยับ | ย่า | ยาว |
|---|-----|-----|-----|------|
|   | *still, yet* | *wrinkled* | *grandma* | *long* |
|   | ยิง | ยิ้ม | ยึด | ยืน |
|   | *to shoot* | *smile* | *to seize* | *to stand* |
|   | ยื่น | เย็น | โยน | ยก |
|   | *to submit* | *cool, cold* | *to throw* | *to lift* |

| น | นะ | นัด | นั่ง | นิ่ม |
|---|-----|-----|------|------|
|   | *final particle* | *appointment* | *to sit* | *soft* |
|   | น้ำ | นิด | แน่ | น้อง |
|   | *aunt* | *tiny* | *certain* | *younger sibling* |

|  |  |  |  |
|---|---|---|---|
| นึก | น้อย | นวด | นิ้ว |
| to think | few | to massage | finger |
| นำ | น้ำ | ใน | เน่า |
| to lead | water | in | rotten |

ณ -

| ร | รับ | ร้าย | ร้าว | รีด |
|---|---|---|---|---|
|  | to receive | bad | cracked | to iron |
|  | เร็ว | แรง | แรก | โรค |
|  | fast | force | first | disease |
|  | รถ | รอ | เรา | ร้อย |
|  | car | to wait | we | hundred |
|  | รวม | ร้อง | เริ่ม | เรียง |
|  | to include | to cry out | to start | to put in order |
|  | เรียน | ร้อน | รวย |  |
|  | to study | hot | rich |  |

| ล | ละ | ลัก | ลัง | ลาก |
|---|---|---|---|---|
|  | per | to steal | box | to drag |
|  | ล่าง | ล้าง | ล้าน | ลึก |
|  | beneath | to wash | million | deep |
|  | ลุก | ลูก | เล็ก | เล็บ |
|  | to get up | one's child | small | nail |
|  | เล่น | เลข | แล้ว | โลก |
|  | to play | number | already | the world |

| ลม | ลด | ลง | ลอง |
|---|---|---|---|
| *wind* | *to reduce* | *to go down* | *to try* |
| เลือก | เลิก | เลี้ยว | เล่า |
| *to choose* | *to quit* | *to turn* | *to tell* |

พ -

| ว | ว่า | ว่าง | | วิ่ง |
|---|---|---|---|---|
| | *to criticize* | *empty, available* | | *to run* |
| | เว้น | วงเวียน | ไว้ | วาง |
| | *to skip* | *roundabout* | *to place something* | *to put something down* |

| ม | มัด | มัน | ม่าน | แม้ |
|---|---|---|---|---|
| | *to tie* | *oily* | *curtain* | *although* |
| | มีด | มุม | เม็ด | มืด |
| | *knife* | *corner* | *pit* | *dark* |
| | มือ | เมือง | โมง | มอง |
| | *hand* | *town* | *o'clock* | *to watch* |
| | มอบ | ไม่ | ไม้ | เมา |
| | *to grant* | *not* | *wood* | *drunk* |
| | แมลง | มี | | |
| | *insect* | *to have* | | |

| หง | เหงา | หงุดหงิด |
|---|---|---|
| | *lonely* | *frustrated* |

| หย | หย่า | หยุด | หยอก | |
|----|------|------|------|---|
| | *to divorce* | *to stop* | *to tease* | |

| หญ | หญ้า | หญิง | ใหญ่ | |
|----|------|------|------|---|
| | *grass* | *female* | *big* | |

| หน | หนา | หน้า | หนัง | หนาว |
|----|------|------|------|------|
| | *thick* | *face* | *movie* | *cold* |
| | หนี | หนู | หนัก | เหนือ |
| | *flee* | *rat* | *heavy* | *north* |
| | หนึ่ง | หน่อย | เหนื่อย | เหนียว |
| | *one* | *little* | *tired* | *sticky* |
| | หนวด | ไหน | | |
| | *moustache* | *which...?* | | |

| หร | หรูหรา | หรือ | เหรียญ | เหรอ |
|----|--------|------|--------|------|
| | *luxurious* | *or* | *coin* | *right?/correct?* |

| หล | หลัง | หลาย | เหล็ก | หลีก |
|----|------|------|-------|------|
| | *behind* | *many* | *steel* | *to avoid* |
| | แหลม | หลับ | โหล | หล่น |
| | *sharp* | *asleep* | *dozen* | *to fall off* |
| | หลง | หลบ | หล่อ | หลอก |
| | *lost (the way)* | *to avoid* | *handsome* | *to deceive* |
| | เหลือ | ไหล | ไหล่ | เหล้า |
| | *to remain* | *to flow* | *shoulder* | *whiskey* |

| หว | หวัด | หวูดหวิด | หวาน | หวัง |
|----|------|----------|------|------|
|    | *a cold* | *almost* | *sweet* | *to hope* |
|    | หวาด | แหวน |  |  |
|    | *be afraid* | *ring* |  |  |

| หม | หมัก | หมา | หมอก | หมี |
|----|------|-----|------|-----|
|    | *to marinate* | *dog* | *fog* | *bear* |
|    | หมิ่น | หมู | หม้าย |  |
|    | *to insult* | *pig* | *a widow* |  |
|    | หมุน | เหม็น | หมึก | หมื่น |
|    | *to spin* | *bad smell* | *ink* | *ten thousand* |
|    | หมด | หมอ | หม้อ | เหมือน |
|    | *to use up* | *doctor* | *pot* | *be alike* |
|    | ไหม้ | ไหม | ใหม่ | เหมาะ |
|    | *burnt* | *silk* | *new* | *suitable* |

## Vocabulary list by vowels

| _ะ | จะ | นะ | ละ | กระเป๋า |
|----|----|----|----|---------|
|    | *will/shall* | *final particle* | *per* | *handbag* |
|    | สะพาน | ทะเล | ถัง | มัน |
|    | *bridge* | *sea* | *bucket* | *it, oily* |
|    | ผัก | รัก | ฟัน | วัน |
|    | *vegetable* | *to love* | *tooth* | *day* |

| _า | ยา | ปลา | ตา | ขา |
|----|----|-----|----|----|
|    | *medicine* | *fish* | *eyes* | *legs* |

ม้า
*horse*

ทาง
*way*

นาย
*Mr., boss*

บิน
*to fly*

นาฬิกา
*clock/watch*

กิน
*to eat*

ผิด
*wrong*

ดิบ
*raw*

สิบ
*ten*

ดี
*good*

ตี
*to strike*

สี
*color*

บีบ
*to squeeze*

รีบ
*hurry*

ซีก
*piece*

ดึง
*to pull*

ครึ่ง
*half*

ตึก
*building*

ปลาหมึก
*squid*

ผึ้ง
*bee*

ถึง
*to arrive*

มือ
*hand*

ถือ
*to carry*

ดื้อ
*stubborn*

หนังสือ
*book*

ซื้อ
*to buy*

หรือ
*or*

มืด
*dark*

จืด
*no flavor*

ยืน
*to stand*

ลื่น
*slippery*

คลื่น
*wave*

พื้น
*floor*

| ◌ุ | ดุ | อายุ | วิทยุ | สุดท้าย |
|---|---|---|---|---|
| | *strict* | *age* | *radio* | *last (adj.)* |
| | ทุก | สุก | | |
| | *every* | *ripe* | | |

| ◌ู | หู | งู | ลูก | ผูก |
|---|---|---|---|---|
| | *ears* | *snake* | *one's child* | *to tie* |
| | ดูด | ถูก | | |
| | *to suck* | *cheap, correct* | | |

| เ◌ะ | เตะ | เละเทะ | เกะกะ | สะเต๊ะ |
|---|---|---|---|---|
| | *to kick* | *messed up* | *disorderly* | *grilled meat* |
| | เอะอะ | เก็บ | เป็ด | เจ็บ |
| | *to make a din* | *to keep* | *duck* | *hurt* |
| | เด็ก | เล็ก | เสร็จ | |
| | *children* | *small* | *finished* | |

| เ◌ | เวลา | เลข | เพศ | เมฆ |
|---|---|---|---|---|
| | *time* | *number* | *gender* | *cloud* |
| | ประเทศ | เหตุ | | |
| | *country* | *cause* | | |

| แ◌ะ | และ | แฉะ | แข็ง | แวะ |
|---|---|---|---|---|
| | *and* | *wet* | *hard* | *to stop by* |
| | แพะ | แตะ | | |
| | *goat* | *to touch* | | |

| แ_ | แพ้ | แดง | แยก | แหวน |
|---|---|---|---|---|
| | to lose | red | to separate | ring |
| | แบบ | แดด | | |
| | style | sun light | | |

| โ_ะ | โต๊ะ | ส้ม | ร่ม | รถ |
|---|---|---|---|---|
| | table/desk | orange | umbrella | car |
| | ยก | สด | ตก | |
| | to lift | fresh | to fall | |

| โ_ | โสด | โมโห | โกรธ | โมง |
|---|---|---|---|---|
| | single | upset | angry | o'clock |
| | กระโดด | โต | | |
| | jump | big | | |

| เ_าะ | เกาะ | เงาะ | เคาะ | เพราะว่า |
|---|---|---|---|---|
| | island | rambutan | to knock | because |
| | เบาะ | เจาะ | นอน | |
| | cushion | to drill | to sleep | |

| _อ | คอ | ขอ | ของ | สอง |
|---|---|---|---|---|
| | throat | to ask for | thing | two |
| | ลอง | จอง | | |
| | to try | to reserve | | |

| เ_อะ | เยอะ | เลอะ | | |
|---|---|---|---|---|
| | *a lot* | *splattered* | | |

| เ_อ | เจอ | เธอ | เดิน | เพิ่ม |
|---|---|---|---|---|
| | *to meet* | *she, you* | *to walk* | *to add* |
| | เริ่ม | เงิน | | |
| | *to start* | *money* | | |

| เ‾ียะ | เปาะเปี๊ยะ | | | |
|---|---|---|---|---|
| | *springroll* | | | |

| เ‾ีย | เสีย | เพลีย | เตี้ย | เรียก |
|---|---|---|---|---|
| | *broken* | *tired* | *short* | *to call* |
| | เกลียด | เที่ยง | | |
| | *to hate* | *noon* | | |

| เ‾ือะ | - | | | |
|---|---|---|---|---|

| เ‾ือ | เสื้อ | เนื้อ | เกลือ | เดือน |
|---|---|---|---|---|
| | *shirt* | *beef* | *salt* | *month* |
| | เพื่อน | เลือก | | |
| | *friend* | *to choose* | | |

| _ัวะ | - | | | |
|---|---|---|---|---|

| ◌ัว | หัวใจ | กลัว | ครัว | สวย |
|---|---|---|---|---|
| | heart | to be afraid of | kitchen | beautiful |
| | รวย | ปวด | | |
| | rich | ache | | |

| ◌ำ | ทำ | กำ | ดำ | ซ้ำ |
|---|---|---|---|---|
| | to do | to grip | black | repeatedly |
| | ย้ำ | น้ำ | | |
| | to emphasize | water | | |

| ใ◌ | ใจ | ใน | | |
|---|---|---|---|---|
| | mind | in | | |

| ไ◌ | ไป | ไกล | ไฟ | ไทย |
|---|---|---|---|---|
| | to go | far | a light, fire | Thai |
| | บันได | ไก่ | ได้ | |
| | stairway | chicken | to get, to be able | |
| | ไม่ | | | |
| | not | | | |

| เ◌า | เช้า | เรา | เมา | ภูเขา |
|---|---|---|---|---|
| | morning | we | drunk | mountain |
| | เท้า | เฝ้า | เท่าไร | |
| | feet | to watch over | how much? | |

## COMPREHENSION EXERCISE

**A. Fill in the gaps using the correct word from the preceding vowel list.**

1. ผม_____ไปทำงาน  ( _ะ )

   *I am going to work.*

2. กางเกง_____ ยาว  ( _า )

   *Long-trousers*

3. ที่นี่มีคนไทย _____ คน  ( _ั )

   *There are ten Thais here.*

4. ผมกำลัง_____  ( _ี )

   *I am in a hurry.*

5. ต้อง_____ไม่ใช่ผลัก  ( _ี )

   *(You) must pull, not push.*

6. เดือนนี้_____เร็ว  ( _ื_ )

   *It gets dark early this month.*

7. คุณ_____เท่าไร?  ( _ุ )

   *How old are you?*

8. ของที่ประเทศไทย_____มาก  ( _ู )

   *Things in Thailand are cheap.*

9. เด็กผู้ชายชอบ_____บอล  ( เ_ะ )

   *Boys like to kick the ball.*

10. คุณมาจาก_____อะไร  ( เ_ )

    *Which country do you come from?*

11. ไม่ชอบเบียร์ใส่น้ำ_____  ( แ_ะ )

    *(I) don't like beer with ice.*

12. ที่กรุงเทพ_____ ติดมาก  ( โ_ะ )

    *Bangkok has heavy traffic jams.*

13. เค้ายังเป็น _____          (โ_)

*She is still single.*

14. _____ภูเก็ตสวยมาก          (เ_าะ)

*Phuket Island is very beautiful.*

15. _____กาแฟสองถ้วย          (_อ)

*May I have two cups of coffee please?*

16. คนไปซื้อของ_____ มาก          (เ_อะ)

*Many people went shopping.*

17. แล้ว_____กัน          (เ_อ)

*See you!*

18. อาหารนี่ _____ แล้ว          (เ◌ย)

*This food is spoiled.*

19. _____ คุณชื่ออะไร?          (เ◌อ)

*What is your friend's name?*

20. ผม _____ งูมาก          (◌ัว)

*I am very afraid of snakes.*

21. ชอบ _____ อะไร?          (◌ำ)

*What do you like to do?*

22. รถอยู่ _____ บ้าน          (ใ_)

*The car is in the house.*

23. ช่วยปิด _____ หน่อยครับ          (ไ_)

*Please turn off the light.*

24. ที่เชียงใหม่มี _____ มาก          (เ_า)

*There are a lot of mountains in Chiang Mai.*

# LESSON 20: Additional Useful Vocabulary

**Action words**

| | | |
|---|---|---|
| กินอาหาร | ทำอาหาร | ทำงาน |
| *to eat* | *to cook* | *to work* |
| ทำความสะอาด | ซื้อของ | ว่ายน้ำ |
| *to clean* | *to do shopping* | *to swim* |
| ประชุม | เล่นกีฬา | ออกกำลังกาย |
| *to have a meeting* | *to play sports* | *to exercise* |
| โทรศัพท์ | ซักผ้า | ได้ยิน |
| *to telephone* | *to do the laundry* | *to hear* |
| จัดของ | รีดผ้า | ล้างจาน |
| *to put things in order* | *to iron* | *to wash dishes* |
| อาบน้ำ | ถ่ายรูป | สนใจ |
| *to bathe, shower* | *to take a picture* | *to be interested in* |

**Qualifiers**

| | | |
|---|---|---|
| อร่อย | สะอาด | สกปรก |
| *delicious* | *clean* | *dirty* |

| เรียบร้อย | ขยัน | ประหยัด |
|---|---|---|
| *neat* | *diligent* | *economical* |

| สบายดี | สบาย | สะดวก |
|---|---|---|
| *fine* | *comfortable* | *convenient* |

| สนุก | ขี้เกียจ | อดทน |
|---|---|---|
| *fun* | *lazy* | *to be patient* |

**Places**

| โรงแรม | โรงเรียน | โรงพยาบาล |
|---|---|---|
| *hotel* | *school* | *hospital* |

| ตึก | ตลาด | ประเทศ |
|---|---|---|
| *building* | *market* | *country* |

| ที่ทำงาน | ห้องประชุม | ที่จอดรถ |
|---|---|---|
| *office* | *meeting room* | *parking lot* |

**Things**

| หนังสือ | หนังสือพิมพ์ | เอกสาร |
|---|---|---|
| *book* | *newspaper* | *document* |

| โทรทัศน์ | กล้องถ่ายรูป | ตู้เย็น |
|---|---|---|
| *television* | *photo camera* | *refrigerator* |

โต๊ะอาหาร
*dining table*

เก้าอี้
*chair*

แอร์
*air conditioner*

ประตู
*door*

หน้าต่าง
*window*

กุญแจ
*key*

เครื่องใช้ไฟฟ้า
*electrical appliance*

เสื้อผ้า
*clothes*

กระเป๋า
*hand bag*

กระโปรง
*skirt*

กางเกง
*trousers*

นาฬิกา
*watch/clock*

ถุงเท้า
*socks*

รองเท้า
*shoes*

เข็มขัด
*belt*

**Question words**

อะไร
*what?*

ที่ไหน
*where?*

เมื่อไร
*when?*

เท่าไร
*how much?*

ใคร
*who?*

ทำไม
*why?*

# LESSON 21: Menus, Forms, Labels, Signs

| รายการอาหาร | **Menu** |
|---|---|
| แกงจืด | *Clear Soup* |
| ผัดผักคะน้าเนื้อน้ำมันหอย | *Stir-fried Kale with Beef in Oyster Sauce* |
| ต้มยำกุ้ง | *Spicy Herbal Soup with Shrimps* |
| ไข่เจียวหมูสับ | *Thai Omelet with Minced Pork* |
| ข้าวผัดอเมริกัน | *American Fried Rice* |
| ส้มตำ | *Papaya Salad* |
| แกงเขียวหวานไก่ | *Green Curry Chicken* |
| ยำทะเล | *Spicy Seafood Salad* |
| หมูทอด | *Deep Fried Pork* |
| ไก่ย่าง | *Grilled Chicken* |
| ทอดมันปลา | *Fish Cake* |
| ข้าวเหนียว | *Sticky Rice* |
| ก๋วยเตี๋ยวน้ำ | *Noodle Soup* |
| เครื่องดื่ม | *Beverage* |
| น้ำผลไม้ | *Fruit Juice* |
| ชาร้อน | *Hot Tea* |

## COMPREHENSION EXERCISE

**A. From the above menu, what would you order.**

1. If you want chicken instead of shrimps in your Spicy Herbal Soup.

2. If you want pork instead of chicken in your Green Curry.

3. If you want beef instead of seafood in your Spicy Salad.

4. If you want deep-fried shrimp.

5. If you want seafood noodle dish.

6. If you want minced chicken instead of pork in your Thai omelet.

7. If you do not want beef in your Stir-fried Kale with Oyster Sauce.

8. If you want grilled pork.

9. If you want orange juice.

10. If you want cold tea with ice.

# แบบฟอร์ม Forms

ชื่อ _____  นามสกุล _____
*Name*  *Last Name*

อายุ _____  วัน _____ เดือน _____ ปี _____
*Age*  *Day*  *Month*  *Year*

เพศ _____  หญิง  ชาย
*Sex*  *Female*  *Male*

วันเกิด ___ / ___ / ___  หมายเลขบัตรประชาชน _____
*Date of Birth*  *ID Number*

เบอร์โทรศัพท์ _____  เบอร์ติดต่อ _____
*Telephone Number*  *Contact Number*

อาชีพ _____
*Occupation*

เงินเดือน _____
*Salary*

ที่อยู่ _____บ้านเลขที่ _____ถนน_____ตำบล _____
*Address*  *House Number*  *Road*  *Sub-District*

อำเภอ_____  จังหวัด _____
*District*  *Province*

วันออกบัตร_____  วันหมดอายุ _____
*Date of Issue*  *Expiry Date*

| ฉลากยา | **Medicine Labels** |
|---|---|
| สรรพคุณ/ประโยชน์ | *Indication/Effect* |
| วิธีรับประทาน/วิธีใช้ | *Dosage* |
| วิธีเก็บรักษา | *Storage Instructions* |
| วันผลิต | *Manufacturing Date* |
| วันหมดอายุ | *Expiry Date* |
| คำเตือน | *Warning* |
| ผลิตโดย | *Manufactured by* |
| ส่วนประกอบ | *Composition* |
| อาการข้างเคียง | *Side Effects* |

## COMPREHENSION EXERCISES

**B. The Thai language borrows and transliterates a number of English words. Many of these loan words contain final consonants that Thais do not pronounce, so they are often spelled using the ' ౯ ' symbol for silent consonants. See if you can spot the English word in each of the following Thai transliterations.**

1. พลาสติก
2. แมนชั่น
3. ไมโครโฟน
4. มอเตอร์ไซด์
5. แฟกซ์
6. โซฟา
7. อพาตเมนท์
8. คอนโดมิเนียม

9. คอมพิวเตอร์

10. วีดีโอ

11. โปสเตอร์

12. แอร์

13. เทป

14. ซีดี

15. แทรกเตอร์

16. บอร์ด

17. การ์ตูน

18. คัทเตอร์

19. แชมพู

20. ดิจิตอล

**C. Some Western food and drinks are simply transliterated into Thai. Determine the English loan words from the list below.**

1. แซนวิชชีส

2. สลัด

3. มักกะโรนี

4. แซนวิช แฮม

5. พิซซ่า

6. ซุบ

7. แฮมเบอร์เกอร์

8. พาสต้า

9. สปาเก็ตตี้

10. ลาซานญ่า

11. เบคอน

12. เฟรนช์ฟรายส์
13. ฮอทดอก
14. ไอศกรีม
15. เค้ก
16. คุกกี้
17. ช็อกโกแล็ต
18. เบียร์
19. ไวน์
20. เป๊ปซี่

## ป้าย   Signs

| Sign | Meaning |
| --- | --- |
| ทางเข้า | Entrance |
| ทางออก | Exit |
| ห้องน้ำ | Toilet |
| ห้องน้ำหญิง | Ladies' Room |
| ห้องน้ำชาย | Mens' Room |
| ห้ามเข้า | No entry |
| ห้ามผ่าน | No passing ahead |
| ห้ามสูบบุหรี่ | No smoking |
| ห้ามกลับรถ | No U-Turn |
| ห้ามกลับรถใต้สะพาน | No U-Turn under the bridge |
| ห้ามเลี้ยวซ้าย | No left turn |
| ห้ามเลี้ยวขวา | No right turn |
| ห้ามจอด | No Parking |
| เลี้ยวซ้ายรอสัญญาณไฟ | No Left on Red (literally: 'Turn left, wait for the traffic light') |
| ทางลัด | Short-cut |
| ซอยตัน | Dead-end Soi |
| ดึง | Pull |
| ผลัก | Push |
| สุวรรณภูมิ | Suvarnabhumi (Airport) |

## COMPREHENSION EXERCISE

**D. Read the signs and answer the questions.**

1. If you want to get out of a garage, which sign should you follow?

    a) ทางเข้า          b) ทางออก

2. If a woman wants to go to the toilet, which sign should she follow?

    a) ห้องน้ำหญิง          b) ห้องน้ำชาย

3. In a restaurant, which sign would you see?

    a) ห้ามกลับรถ          b) ห้ามสูบบุหรี่

4. If you want to get a taxi, which sign should you look for?

    a) ห้ามจอด          b) ที่จอดรถแท็กซี่

5. Which sign represents 'one way street'?

    a) เดินรถทางเดียว          b) ห้ามเลี้ยว

6. Which sign tells you to wait for the traffic light?

    a) เลี้ยวซ้ายผ่านตลอด          b) เลี้ยวซ้ายรอสัญญาณไฟ

7. You are looking for a short - cut, which sign would you follow?

    a) ทางลัด          b) ซอยตัน

8. Which sign tells you to U-turn?

    a) กลับรถใต้สะพาน          b) ห้ามกลับรถ

# LESSON 22: CALENDAR AND GEOGRAPHY

## วัน    Days

| Word | Pronunciation | Meaning |
|------|---------------|---------|
| วันอาทิตย์ | วัน-อา-ทิด | *Sunday* |
| วันจันทร์ | วัน-จัน | *Monday* |
| วันอังคาร | วัน-อัง-คาน | *Tuesday* |
| วันพุธ | วัน-พุด | *Wednesday* |
| วันพฤหัสบดี | วัน-พรึ-หัด-สะ-บอ-ดี | *Thursday* |
| วันศุกร์ | วัน-สุก | *Friday* |
| วันเสาร์ | วัน-เสา | *Saturday* |
| วันหยุดสุดสัปดาห์ | วัน-หยุด-สุด-สับ-ดา | *Weekend* |
| วันทำงาน | วัน-ทำ-งาน | *Working Day* |
| วันหยุด | วัน-หยุด | *Holiday* |
| วันเกิด | วัน-เกิด | *Birthday* |
| วันแต่งงาน | วัน-แต่ง-งาน | *Wedding Day* |
| วันขึ้นปีใหม่ | วัน-ขึ้น-ปี-ใหม่ | *New Year's Day* |
| วันครบรอบ | วัน-ครบ-รอบ | *Anniversary* |
| วันแม่ | วัน-แม่ | *Mother's Day* |
| วันพ่อ | วัน-พ่อ | *Father's Day* |
| วันวาเลนไทน์ | วัน-วา-เลน-ไท | *Valentine's Day* |
| วันสงกรานต์ | วัน-สง-กราน | *Songkran Day* |
| วันคริสต์มาส | วัน-คริด-สะ-มาด | *Christmas Day* |
| วันที่ | วัน-ที่ | *Date* |

## เดือน    Months

| Word | Pronunciation | Meaning |
|------|---------------|---------|
| มกราคม | มก-กะ-รา-คม | *January* |
| กุมภาพันธ์ | กุม-พา-พัน | *February* |
| มีนาคม | มี-นา-คม | *March* |
| เมษายน | เม-สา-ยน | *April* |
| พฤษภาคม | พรึด-สะ-พา-คม | *May* |
| มิถุนายน | มิ-ถุ-นา-ยน | *June* |
| กรกฎาคม | กะ-ระ-กะ-ดา-คม | *July* |
| สิงหาคม | สิง-หา-คม | *August* |
| กันยายน | กัน-ยา-ยน | *September* |
| ตุลาคม | ตุ-ลา-คม | *October* |
| พฤศจิกายน | พรึด-สะ-จิ-กา-ยน | *November* |
| ธันวาคม | ทัน-วา-คม | *December* |

## COMPREHENSION EXERCISE

### A. Answer the questions.

1. วันที่ 1 เดือน มกราคมเป็นวันอะไร?
2. เดือนอะไรมี 30 วัน?
3. เดือนอะไรมี 31 วัน?
4. เดือนอะไรมี 28 วัน?
5. วันสงกรานต์อยู่ในเดือนอะไร?
6. วันคริสต์มาสอยู่ในเดือนอะไร?
7. วันพ่อของประเทศไทยเป็นวันที่เท่าไร?
8. วันแม่ของประเทศไทยเป็นวันที่เท่าไร?
9. วันวาเลนไทน์อยู่ในเดือนอะไร?

Since there is no universal standard for transliterating Thai into English, the names of provinces, roads, buildings, etc. are often spelled in a variety of ways, causing confusion to foreigners. The following lists show the names of all provinces in Thailand and some main roads in Bangkok, which you may encounter elsewhere spelled somewhat differently in English.

## จังหวัดในประเทศไทย Provinces of Thailand

### ภาคกลาง The Central Region

| Province | Pronunciation | Transliteration |
|---|---|---|
| กรุงเทพมหานคร | กรุง-เทบ-มะ-หา-นะ-คอน | Bangkok |
| ฉะเชิงเทรา | ฉะ-เชิง-เซา | Chachoengsao |
| กาญจนบุรี | กาน-จะ-นะ-บุ-รี | Kanchanaburi |
| ชัยนาท | ชัย-นาด | Chainat |
| นนทบุรี | นน-ทะ-บุ-รี | Nonthaburi |
| นครปฐม | นะ-คอน-ปะ-ถม | Nakhon Pathom |
| นครนายก | นะ-คอน-นา-ยก | Nakhon Nayok |
| ปทุมธานี | ปะ-ทุม-ทา-นี | Pathum Thani |
| ประจวบคีรีขันธ์ | ประ-จวบ-คี-รี-ขัน | Prachuap Khirikhan |
| ปราจีนบุรี | ปรา-จีน-บุ-รี | Prachin Buri |
| เพชรบุรี | เพ็ด-ชะ-บุ-รี | Petch Buri |
| ราชบุรี | ราด-ชะ-บุ-รี | Ratchaburi |
| ลพบุรี | ลบ-บุ-รี | Lop Buri |
| สมุทรปราการ | สะ-หมุด-ปรา-กาน | Samut Prakan |
| สมุทรสาคร | สะ-หมุด-สา-คอน | Samut Sakhon |
| สมุทรสงคราม | สะ-หมุด-สง-คราม | Samut Songkhram |

| สระบุรี | สะ-หระ-บุ-รี | *Saraburi* |
| สิงห์บุรี | สิง-บุ-รี | *Sing Buri* |
| สุพรรณบุรี | สุ-พัน-บุ-รี | *Suphan Buri* |
| สระแก้ว | สะ-แก้ว | *Sa Kaeo* |
| อ่างทอง | อ่าง-ทอง | *Ang Thong* |
| อยุธยา | อะ-ยุด-ทะ-ยา | *Ayutthaya* |

## ภาคเหนือ  The Northern Region

| Province | Pronunciation | Transliteration |
| --- | --- | --- |
| กำแพงเพชร | กำ-แพง-เพ็ด | *Kampaeng Phet* |
| เชียงใหม่ | เชียง-ใหม่ | *Chiang Mai* |
| เชียงราย | เชียง-ราย | *Chiang Rai* |
| ตาก | ตาก | *Tak* |
| นครสวรรค์ | นะ-คอน-สะ-หวัน | *Nakhon Sawan* |
| น่าน | น่าน | *Nan* |
| พะเยา | พะ-เยา | *Phayao* |
| พิจิตร | พิ-จิด | *Phichit* |
| พิษณุโลก | พิด-สะ-นุ-โลก | *Phitsanulok* |
| เพชรบูรณ์ | เพ็ด-ชะ-บูน | *Phetchabun* |
| แพร่ | แพร่ | *Phrae* |
| แม่ฮ่องสอน | แม่-ห้อง-สอน | *Mae Hong Son* |
| ลำปาง | ลำ-ปาง | *Lampang* |
| ลำพูน | ลำ-พูน | *Lamphun* |
| สุโขทัย | สุ-โข-ทัย | *Sukhothai* |
| อุทัยธานี | อุ-ทัย-ทา-นี | *Uthai Thani* |
| อุตรดิตถ์ | อุด-ตะ-ระ-ดิด | *Uttaradit* |

## ภาคอีสาน  The Northeastern Region

| Province | Pronunciation | Transliteration |
|---|---|---|
| กาฬสินธ์ | กา-ละ-สิน | *Kalasin* |
| ขอนแก่น | ขอน-แก่น | *Khon Kaen* |
| ชัยภูมิ | ชัย-ยะ-พูม | *Chaiyaphum* |
| นครราชสีมา | นะ-คอน-ราด-ชะ-สี-มา | *Nakhon Ratchasima* |
| นครพนม | นะ-คอน-พะ-นม | *Nakhon Phanom* |
| บุรีรัมย์ | บุ-รี-รัม | *Buri Ram* |
| มหาสารคาม | มะ-หา-สา-ระ-คาม | *Maha Sarakham* |
| มุกดาหาร | มุก-ดา-หาน | *Mukdahan* |
| ยโสธร | ยะ-โส-ทอน | *Yasothon* |
| ร้อยเอ็ด | ร้อย- เอ็ด | *Roi Et* |
| เลย | เลย | *Loei* |
| ศรีสะเกษ | สี-สะ-เกด | *Si Sa Ket* |
| สกลนคร | สะ-กน-นะ-คอน | *Sakhon Nakhon* |
| สุรินทร์ | สุ-ริน | *Surin* |
| หนองคาย | หนอง-คาย | *Nong Khai* |
| หนองบัวลำภู | หนอง-บัว-ลำ-พู | *Nong Bua Lum Phu* |
| อุดรธานี | อุ-ดอน-ทา-นี | *Udon Thani* |
| อุบลราชธานี | อุ-บน-ราด-ชะ-ทา-นี | *Ubon Ratchathani* |
| อำนาจเจริญ | อำ-นาด-จะ-เริน | *Amnat Charoen* |

## ภาคตะวันออก  The Eastern Region

| Province | Pronunciation | Transliteration |
|---|---|---|
| จันทบุรี | จัน-ทะ-บุ-รี | *Chanthaburi* |
| ชลบุรี | ชน-บุ-รี | *Chon Buri* |
| ตราด | ตราด | *Trad* |

| ระยอง | ระ-ยอง | *Rayong* |

## ภาคใต้ The Southern Region

| Province | Pronunciation | Transliteration |
|---|---|---|
| กระบี่ | กระ-บี่ | *Krabi* |
| ชุมพร | ชุม-พอน | *Chumphon* |
| ตรัง | ตรัง | *Trang* |
| นราธิวาส | นะ-รา-ทิ-วาด | *Narathiwat* |
| นครศรีธรรมราช | นะ-คอน-สี-ทำ-มะ-ราด | *Nakhon Si Thammarat* |
| ปัตตานี | ปัด-ตา-นี | *Pattani* |
| พัทลุง | พัด-ทะ-ลุง | *Phatthalung* |
| พังงา | พัง-งา | *Phang-nga* |
| ภูเก็ต | พู-เก็ด | *Phuket* |
| ยะลา | ยะ-ลา | *Yala* |
| ระนอง | ระ-นอง | *Ranong* |
| สตูล | สะ-ตูน | *Satun* |
| สงขลา | สง-ขลา | *Songkhla* |
| สุราษฎร์ธานี | สุ-ราด-ทา-นี | *Suratthani* |

## รายชื่อถนนบางสายในกรุงเทพ Main Roads in Bangkok

| Street | Pronunciation | Transliteration |
|---|---|---|
| สุขุมวิท | สุ-ขุม-วิด | *Sukhumvit* |
| อโศก | อะ-โสก | *Asoke* |
| รัชดาภิเษก | รัด-ชะ-ดา-พิ-เสก | *Ratchdapisek* |
| เพชรเกษม | เพ็ด-ชะ-กะ-เสม | *Petchkasem* |
| พหลโยธิน | พะ-หน-โย-ทิน | *Phahol-yothin* |

| พระราม 4 | พระ-ราม-สี่ | Pra-raam 4 OR Rama 4 |
| สาทรเหนือ | สา-ทอน-เหนือ | Sathon Nua |
| สาทรใต้ | สา-ทอน-ใต้ | Sathon Tai |
| สวนพลู | สวน-พลู | Suanplu |
| วิทยุ | วิด-ทะ-ยุ | Wittayu OR Wireless |
| เพลินจิต | เพลิน-จิด | Ploenchit |
| สารสิน | สา-ระ-สิน | Sarasin |
| นราธิวาส | นะ-รา-ทิ-วาด | Naratiwat |
| สีลม | สี-ลม | Silom |
| เจริญกรุง | จะ-เริน-กรุง | Chareonkrung OR New Road |
| ราชวิถี | ราด-ชะ-วิ-ถี | Ratchvithi |
| ราชดำเนิน | ราด-ชะ-ดำ-เนิน | Ratchdamnoen |
| บางนา | บาง-นา | Bangna |
| พญาไท | พะ-ยา-ไท | Phyathai |
| ศรีอยุธยา | สี-อะ-ยุด-ทะ-ยา | Sri Ayutthaya |
| กำแพงเพชร | กำ-แพง-เพ็ด | Kampaengpetch |
| วิภาวดีรังสิต | วิ-พา-วะ-ดี-รัง-สิด | Vipavadii Rangsit |
| งามวงศ์วาน | งาม-วง-วาน | Ngamwongwan |
| แจ้งวัฒนะ | แจ้ง-วัด-ทะ-นะ | Jaengwattana |
| พิษณุโลก | พิด-สะ-นุ-โลก | Pitsanuloke |
| สุโขทัย | สุ-โข-ทัย | Sukhothai |
| เยาวราช | เยา-วะ-ราด | Yaowarat |
| บำรุงเมือง | บำ-รุง-เมือง | Bumrungmuang |

## COMPREHENSION EXERCISE

## B. Which countries are listed below?

1. ออสเตรเลีย
2. มาเลเซีย
3. สเปน
4. รัสเซีย
5. อิตาลี
6. โคลัมเบีย
7. ชิลี
8. อเมริกา
9. บรูไน
10. อิรัก
11. ซูดาน
12. สิงคโปร์
13. เวียดนาม
14. คานาดา
15. อินเดีย

# LESSON 23: Questions, Games, Crosswords

**A. Match the words in the middle column with those in the right column to form the compound Thai words with the same meaning as the English word in the left column.**

| | | |
|---|---|---|
| 1.  hotel | โรง | a ) นาย |
| 2.  student | นัก | b ) แรม |
| 3.  shoes | รอง | c ) ตก |
| 4.  mattress | ที่ | d ) เท้า |
| 5.  walkway | ทาง | e ) ครัว |
| 6.  toilet | ห้อง | f ) เรียน |
| 7.  waterfall | น้ำ | g ) น้ำ |
| 8.  chef | พ่อ | h ) เดิน |
| 9.  boss | เจ้า | i ) นอน |
| 10. restaurant | ร้าน | j ) อาหาร |

**B. Read and choose the right answer.**

1. กาแฟ  is

    a) food 　　　　　 b) drink 　　　　　 c) place

2. ข้าวผัด  is

    a) food 　　　　　 b) drink 　　　　　 c) place

3. โรงแรม  is

    a) food 　　　　　 b) drink 　　　　　 c) place

4. สุขุมวิท  is

    a) place 　　　　　 b) road 　　　　　 c) country

153

5. บาท is

   a) place                  b) money               c) food

6. เจ้าพระยา is

   a) place                  b) mountain         c) river

7. กรุงเทพ is

   a) country              b) capital             c) ocean

8. มอเตอร์ไซค์ is

   a) town                   b) transport         c) action

9. มาเลเซีย is

   a) country              b) capital             c) continent

## C. Word Puzzle

| ก | ง | า | จ | อ | ง |
|---|---|---|---|---|---|
| ป | ม | ท | อ | ด | า |
| ห | บ | ถ | ด | จ | น |
| ฒ | อ | า | ห | า | ร |
| ซ | ล | ม | น | น | ถ |
| ต | อ | บ | ย | ว | ห |

1. to reserve    __ __ ง          2. plate       จ __ __

3. food        __ __ __ ร       4. job        __ น

5. market    ต __ __ __        6. to park    __ อ __

7. dog      __ ม __            8. car        __ __

9. deep fried    __ __ ด      10. to ask    __ า __

11. long time    __ า __       12. to answer    __ อ __

## D. Find the matching synonyms in Thai.

| | | |
|---|---|---|
| 1. ไม่อ้วน | a ) ยาว | |
| 2. ไม่สะอาด | b ) หิว | |
| 3. ไม่เตี้ย | c ) แพง | |
| 4. ไม่อิ่ม | d ) ป่วย | |
| 5. ไม่สบาย | e ) ง่าย | |
| 6. ไม่ยาก | f ) ร้อน | |
| 7. ไม่หนาว | g ) ผอม | |
| 8. ไม่ถูก | h ) สูง | |
| 9. ไม่สั้น | i ) สกปรก | |
| 10. ไม่เร็ว | j ) ยุ่ง | |
| 11. ไม่ว่าง | k ) ดัง | |
| 12. ไม่เงียบ | l ) ช้า | |

## E. Find the corresponding anonyms in Thai.

| | | |
|---|---|---|
| 1. หน้า | a ) หลับ | |
| 2. ซ้าย | b ) ขวา | |
| 3. บน | c ) หลัง | |
| 4. ข้างนอก | d ) ช้า | |
| 5. เข้า | e ) มาก | |
| 6. ขาว | f ) ข้างใน | |
| 7. ใหญ่ | g ) ออก | |
| 8. น้อย | h ) ล่าง | |
| 9. เร็ว | i ) ดำ | |
| 10. ตื่น | j ) เล็ก | |
| 11. ไกล | k ) เบา | |
| 12. หนัก | l ) ใกล้ | |

**F. Find the correct missing words.**

1. คนไทยพูด_____ไทย      a ) ชื่อ
    *Thai people speak Thai language.*

2. กรุงเทพ_____เมืองหลวงของประเทศไทย      b ) มา
    *Bangkok is Thailand's capital.*

3. เชียงใหม่_____ภาคเหนือ      c ) เป็น
    *Chiang Mai is in the northern region.*

4. คุณ_____จากที่ไหน?      d ) ภาษา
    *Where do you come from?*

5. ผมชอบ_____อาหารไทย      e ) ดู
    *I like to eat Thai food.*

6. เราไม่_____ไปอยุธยา      f ) เดิน
    *We have never been to Ayutthaya.*

7. ฉัน_____มาทำงานทุกวัน      g ) อยู่
    *I walk to work everyday.*

8. ช่วย _____ประตูหน่อยค่ะ      h ) เคย
    *Could you please open the door?*

9. ลูกคุณจิม_____อะไร?      i ) ทาน
    *What is the name of Jim's son?*

10. ไม่ชอบ_____ทีวี      j ) เปิด
    *(I) don't like to watch T.V.*

**G. Choose the correct answer.**

1. คนไทยกิน_____ทุกวัน      *Thai people eat rice everyday.*

     a) ขาว          b) ข่าว          c) ข้าว

2. ใส่_____สีแดง    *To wear a red shirt.*

    a) เสื้อ          b) เสื่อ          c) เสือ

3. หนึ่ง สอง สาม สี่ _____    *One Two Three Four Five*

    a) หา          b) ห้า          c) ห่า

4. _____น้ำหนึ่งขวดหน่อยค่ะ    *May I have a bottle of water please?*

    a) คอ          b) ข้อ          c) ขอ

5. คุณ_____ถึงเมื่อไร?    *When did you arrive?*

    a) มา          b) หมา          c) ม้า

6. ใคร_____ไปเที่ยว?    *Who wants to go out?*

    a) อยาก          b) ยาก          c) หยาก

7. ถ้าไม่สบายต้องกิน_____    *If (you) are sick, (you) must take medicine.*

    a) ยา          b) หย่า          c) ย่า

8. คุณพูดไม่ถูก คุณพูด_____    *You did not speak correctly, you spoke wrong.*

    a) ผิด          b) ปิด          c) พิด

9. ดำ ขาว เขียว แดง เป็น _____    *Black, white, green and red are colors.*

    a) สี่          b) สี          c) สี้

10. อาหารที่นี่ _____มาก    *The food here is very fresh.*

    a) สด          b) ซด          c) โสด

## H. Cross Word

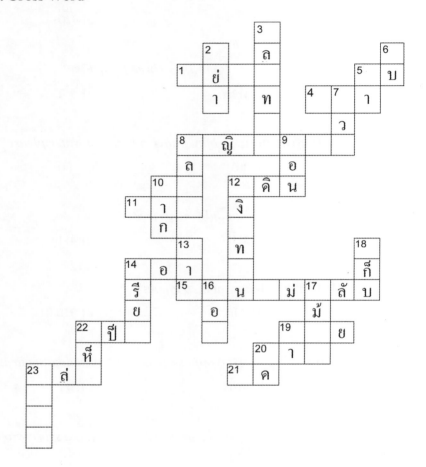

**Across** 1. kind  4. we  5. to meet  8. beautiful woman  10. to come  11. shy
12. to walk  14. to want  15. can't sleep  19. something is lost  20. late  21. bland
flavor  22. to be  23. to play

**Down** 2. Don't  3. lost the way  5. to bring someone to somewhere  6. secret
7. rich  8. many  9. to teach  10. a lot  12. changes (money)  13. to read  14. to
study  16. out  17. widow  18. to keep  20. fresh  22. to see  23. to write

## I. Cross Word

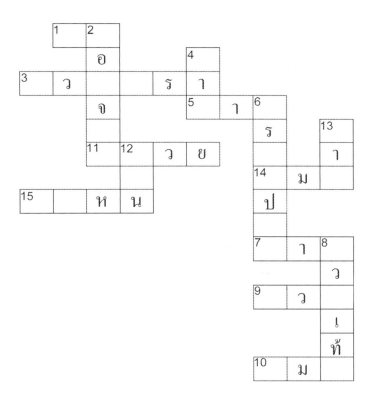

**Across** 1. to buy  3. we  5. difficult  7. job  9. ache  10. dog  11. banana
14. o'clock  15. where?

**Down**  2. to leave  4. to sell  6. skirt  8. foot massage  12. million  13. way

## J. Cross Word

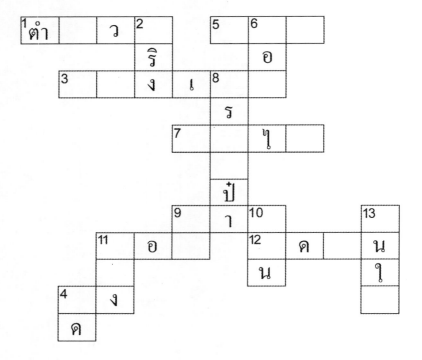

**Across**  1. police  3. trousers  4. to go down  5. finished, no more  7. What?
9. plate  11. hot  12. to be patient

**Down**  2. real  4. to reduce  6. to look  8. bag  10. to sleep  11. to cry out
13. to be interested in

## K. Put the consonants and the vowels in the right order.

1. what      ะ ไ ร อ      _ _ _ _

2. where      ห ท น ไ ' ◌ี      _ ไ _ _

3. when      ◌ี ' อ เ ไ ร ม      _ _ _ ไ _

4. why      ◌ำ ท ม ไ      _ _ ไ _

5. how much      ' า เ ไ ท ร      _ _ า _ ร

6. food      า ห ร อ า      อ _ ห _ _

7. fine      ◌ี บ า ส ด ย      ส _ _ ย _

8. see      ห น เ ◌ี      _ _ น

9. rice      า ◌ู ข ว      _ _ ว

10. cheap      ◌ุ ถ ก      _ ก

11. expensive      ง แ พ      _ _ ง

12. like      อ ช บ      ช _ _

13. friend      ◌ี อ น เ ' พ      _ พ _ _

14. spicy           เ ค ผ ็                  _ _ ค

15. hot             อ ร ้ น                  _ _น

16. appointment     ั ด น                  น _

17. late            า ส ย                  _ _ ย

18. meet           อ เ จ                  เ _ _

19. stay            ุ ่ อ ย                  อ _

# PART 2

PART 2

# LESSON 24: HOW TO FORM PHRASES
## AND SENTENCES

To create a phrase or a sentence, you need to know the basic rules of grammar. Thai grammar is generally much less complicated than English grammar. The key rules are listed below.

**1. Pronouns and Final Particles:** Thais use their pronouns variably according to their status, age, gender, position, profession, etc. In general,

    ผม    is used as '*I, me*' for men

    ดิฉัน is used as '*I, me*' for women

    คุณ  is used for '*you*'

    เขา or เค้า is for the third person '*she, he, her, him*'

    พวกเขา or พวกเค้า is for '*they, them*'

    พวกเรา is for '*we, us*'

Apart from using different pronouns, different genders also use different polite particles to end a sentence. Women say 'คะ' at the end of a statement and 'คะ' at the end of a question. Men only say 'ครับ' both at the end of statements and questions (sometimes you may hear 'คลับ' or 'คับ'). When Thais address each other, they will use first names preceded by the word คุณ (similar to 'Mr.', 'Ms.'), by a title, or by other status-related words (e.g., 'brother', 'sister').

In informal circumstances, Thais often address each other by using a family status pronoun, even though they are not actually related. In colloquial

Thai, it is customary to leave out the pronouns 'you' and 'I', prepositions and some other words, provided that the intended meaning of the sentence is expressed adequately.

**2. Possession:** Ownership is indicated by adding the word ของ after the thing being possessed and before the possessor, but this word is often omitted.

**Examples:**

| | |
|---|---|
| ห้อง(ของ)ผม | *my room* |
| บ้าน(ของ)เรา | *our house* |

**3. Plurality:** There are no articles in front of nouns and there is no distinction in form between singular and plural. Plurality is indicated by the context or by additional words, such as quantifiers.

**Examples:**

| | |
|---|---|
| เค้ามีรถ | *I have a car/cars.* |
| เค้ามีรถสี่คัน | *I have 4 cars.* |

**4. Classifiers:** As you can see from the examples above, when quantifying a noun, the amount comes after the noun but before its classifier. Classifiers are words used to specify the unit of items, things, living beings, etc.

A classifier is required when you want to identify a quantity of something. Some nouns are used as their own classifier; e.g. ห้อง *room*, คน *person*. Nouns that share similar features use the same classifiers. The next table lists the most commonly used classifiers:

**Table of Classifiers**

| Nouns | Classifiers |
|---|---|
| Persons | คน |
| Animals, Tables, Desks, Chairs, Clothes | ตัว |
| Anything in pairs | คู่ |
| Anything round | ลูก |
| Anything flat and thin | แผ่น |
| Electronic appliances | เครื่อง |
| Cars, Land vehicles | คัน |
| Small items in general | อัน |
| Books | เล่ม |

**5. Inflection:** The verb in Thai does not change its form to correlate with changes in nouns, pronouns, or time. However, the context usually makes it clear which interpretation is intended, sometimes by the use of extra words. The time or state of an action is indicated by the use of time words and/or particles. The future tense is indicated by putting the word ' จะ ' directly in front of the verb.

**Examples:**

| | |
|---|---|
| เค้าทำงานที่นี่ | *He/she works here.* |
| พวกเค้าทำงานที่นี่ | *They work here.* |
| ตอนนี้ผมทำงานที่กรุงเทพ | *Presently, I work in Bangkok.* |

เมื่อก่อนนี้ผมทำงานที่กรุงเทพ         *Previously, I worked in Bangkok.*

ผมจะทำงานที่กรุงเทพ                 *I will work in Bangkok.*

**6. Word Order:** Adjectives and specific names come after the nouns they modify, not before as in English.

**Examples:**

คนสวย                              *(a) beautiful person*

ประเทศเล็ก                          *(a) small country*

ภาษาไทย                            *Thai language*

โรงแรมฮิวตัน                         *Hilton Hotel*

**7. Basic Sentence Structure:**

**7.1** The basic English structure: Subject + 'to be' + adjective, when converted into Thai, 'to be' is always omitted.

**Examples:**

บ้านสะอาด                          *The house is clean.*

อากาศเย็น                           *The weather is cool.*

อาหารเผ็ด                           *The food is spicy.*

**7.2** There are principally two words: 'เป็น' and 'อยู่' which are equivalent to 'to be' in English. In Thai, these two words are mainly used before a noun.

'เป็น' is used to state one's nationality, career or relationship

'อยู่'  is used to state one's location.

**Examples:**

คุณเป็นคนไทย                        *You are Thai.*

| | |
|---|---|
| คุณแซมเป็นสามีดิฉัน | *Khun Sam is my husband.* |
| คุณเล็กเป็นหมอ | *Khun Lek is a doctor.* |
| เค้าอยู่เชียงใหม่ | *He/she lives in Chiang Mai.* |
| เชียงใหม่อยู่ภาคเหนือ | *Chiang Mai is in the northern region.* |

**7.3**  The basic structure of a Thai sentence (including a question) is Subject + Verb + Object.

**Examples:**

| | |
|---|---|
| เค้าชอบทำอาหาร | *He/she likes to cook.* |
| เค้าชอบทำอาหารกับเพื่อน | *He/she likes to cook with friends.* |
| เค้าชอบทำอาหารกับเพื่อน | *He/she likes to cook with* |
| ที่บ้านทุกวันพุธ | *friends at home every Wednesday.* |

**7.4**  In general, a question can be formed by inserting a question word at the position where you need an answer. The question word for a yes-no question is usually placed at the end of the sentence.

**Table of Question Words**

| Question Words | English Equivalents |
|---|---|
| 1. อะไร? | What? |
| 2. ที่ไหน? | Where? |
| 3. เมื่อไร? | When? |
| 4. ใคร? | Who? |
| 5. ยังไง? ( อย่างไร?) | How? |

| | |
|---|---|
| 6. เท่าไร? | How much? |
| 7. ทำไม? | Why? |
| 8. มั้ย? (ไหม?) | Do, does, is, am, are? |
| 9. รึเปล่า? (หรือเปล่า?) | Do, does, is, am, are? |
| 10. แล้วรึยัง? or รึยัง? or ยัง? (แล้วหรือยัง?) | Have...already or not yet? |
| 11. เคย......แล้วรึยัง? | Have...ever...before? |
| 12. ได้มั้ย? (ได้ไหม?) | Can? |
| 13. เหรอ? (หรือ?) | Right? (confirmation) |
| 14. ใช่มั้ย? (ใช่ไหม?) | Right? (confirmation) |
| 15. กี่ + classifier? | How many..? |
| 16. classifier + ไหน? | Which..? |

The following questions are transformed from the statements shown in section 7.3. Observe the word order.

**Examples:**

เค้าชอบทำอาหารอะไร?

*What does he/she like to cook?*

เค้าชอบทำอาหารกับใคร?

*Who does he/she like to cook with?*

เค้าชอบทำอาหารกับเพื่อนที่ไหน?
*Where does he/she like to cook with friends?*

ใครชอบทำอาหารกับเพื่อนที่บ้าน?
*Who likes to cook with friends at home?*

เค้าชอบทำอาหารกับเพื่อนเมื่อไร?
*When does he/she like to cook with friends at home?*

เค้าชอบทำอาหารกับเพื่อนรึเปล่า?
*Does he/she like to cook with friends?*

เค้าชอบทำอาหารกับเพื่อนมั้ย?
*Does he/she like to cook with friends?*

เค้าทำอาหารแล้วรึยัง?
*Has he/she already cooked or not yet?*

เค้าเคยทำอาหารกับเพื่อนแล้วรึยัง?
*Has he/she ever cooked with his/her friends?*

เค้าชอบทำอาหารกับเพื่อนใช่มั้ย?
*He/she likes to cook with friends, doesn't he/she?*

เค้าชอบทำอาหารกับเพื่อนเหรอ?
*He/she likes to cook with friends, doesn't he/she?*

เค้าทำอาหารได้มั้ย?

*Can he/she cook?*

เค้าชอบทำอาหารกี่อย่าง?

*How many kinds of food does he/she like to cook?*

**7.5** Possible answers to the question words given in the table in section 7.4:

7.5.1 To answer the question words 1- 6, you may simply say the answers without repeating the whole sentence.

7.5.2 To answer question word 'ทำไม?' (7), you may start with เพราะว่า meaning 'because'.

7.5.3 To answer question words 'มั้ย?' (8) & 'รึเปล่า?' (9), you may repeat the key word(s) when the answer is affirmative. When the answer is negative, put 'ไม่' in front of the key word(s).

**Examples:**

**Question 1**  เค้าชอบทำอาหารกับเพื่อนรึเปล่า?

*Does he/she like to cook with friends?*

**Answers**  ชอบ  *Yes*

ไม่ชอบ  *No*

**Question 2**  อาหารอร่อยมั้ย?

*Is the food delicious?*

**Answers**  อร่อย  *Yes*

ไม่อร่อย  *No*

**7.5.4** To answer question words 'แล้วรึยัง?' or 'รึยัง?' or 'ยัง?' (10), you may repeat the key word(s) + 'แล้ว', when the answer is affirmative.When the answer is negative, say 'ยังไม่' + the key word(s), or 'ยัง' in short.

**Examples:**

**Question 1**    เค้าทำอาหาร แล้วรึยัง?

               *Has he/she cooked already or not yet?*

**Answers**    ทำ แล้ว      *Yes, already.*

               ยังไม่ทำ     *Not yet.*

               ยัง           *Not yet.*

**Question 2**    คุณอ่านหนังสือพิมพ์วันนี้แล้วรึยัง?

               *Have you read today's newspaper already?*

**Answers**    อ่านแล้ว     *Yes, already.*

               ยังไม่อ่าน    *Not yet.*

               ยัง           *Not yet.*


**7.5.5** To answer question words 'เคย...... แล้วรึยัง ?' (11), you may simply say 'เคย แล้ว', when the answer is affirmative.When the answer is negative, say 'ยังไม่ เคย', or 'ยัง' in short.

**Examples:**

**Question1**    เค้าเคยทำอาหาร แล้วรึยัง?

               *Has he/she ever cooked before?*

**Answers**    เคยแล้ว     *Yes, already.*

               ยังไม่เคย    *Not yet.*

               ยัง           *Not yet.*

**Question 2** คุณเคยอ่าน Bangkok Post แล้วรึยัง?

*Have you ever read the Bangkok Post?*

**Answers** เคยแล้ว     *Yes, already.*

ยังไม่เคย     *Not yet.*

ยัง     *Not yet.*

7.5.6 To answer question word 'ได้มั้ย?' (12), say 'ได้' when the answer is affirmative. When the answer is negative, say 'ไม่ได้'.

**Example:**

**Question 1** เค้าทำอาหารได้มั้ย?

*Can he/she cook?*

**Answers** ได้     *Yes*

ไม่ได้     *No*

7.5.7 To answer question words 'เหรอ?' (13) & 'ใช่มั้ย?' (14), say 'ใช่' when the answer is affirmative. When the answer is negative, say 'ไม่ใช่' or 'เปล่า'.

**Examples:**

**Question 1** เค้าชอบทำอาหารกับเพื่อนเหรอ?

*Does he/she like to cook with friends?*

**Answers** ใช่     *Yes*

ไม่ใช่     *No*

เปล่า     *No*

**Question 2** คุณเป็นคนไทยใช่มั้ย?

*Are you Thai?*

**Answers**    ใช่          *Yes*

                ไม่ใช่        *No*

                เปล่า        *No*

**7.5.8** To answer question words 'กี่'+ classifier? (15), say the amount followed by the classifier.

**Example:**

**Question 1**  เค้าชอบทำอาหารกี่อย่าง?

                *How many kinds of food does he/she like to cook?*

**Answer**      สี่อย่าง      *Four kinds.*

**7.5.9** To answer question words classifier + 'ไหน?' (16), you may repeat the classifier followed by the answer.

**Examples:**

**Question 1**  ระหว่างเสื้อสีแดงกับสีเขียวคุณชอบตัวไหน?

                *Between the red shirt and the green shirt,*

                *which one do you like?*

**Answer**      ตัวสีแดง     *The red one.*

**Question 2**  คุณอยากได้รถคันไหน?

                *Which car would you like to have?*

**Answer**      คันนั้น       *That one.*

**7.6** A negative sentence is formed by putting a negative word in front of the verb, such as 'ไม่' (*not*), or 'ไม่ได้' (*did not, not being*).

**Examples:**

เราไม่ดื่มกาแฟ                              *We don't drink coffee.*

| | |
|---|---|
| เค้าไม่ได้เรียน | *He/She didn't study.* |
| ผมไม่ได้เป็นคนอังกฤษ | *I am not English.* |

'ไม่ได้', when placed after a verb or at the end of a sentence, means '*can't*'. However, when it precedes a verb, it means '*didn't*'.

**Examples**:

| | |
|---|---|
| ผมพูดภาษาไทยไม่ได้ | *I can't speak Thai.* |
| วันนี้ผมไปทำงานไม่ได้ | *I can't go to work today.* |
| วันนี้ผมไม่ได้ไปทำงาน | *I didn't go to work today.* |

'ไม่เป็น' can also be used at the end of a sentence, but the meaning is limited to '*not able to due to lack of knowledge*'.

**Examples**:

| | |
|---|---|
| ผมพูดภาษาไทยไม่เป็น | *I can't speak Thai.* |
| ผมอ่านภาษาอังกฤษไม่เป็น | *I can't read English.* |

8. **Negative Qualifiers:** When a negative word qualifies an adjective or an adverb in Thai, it is usually placed between the noun and the adjective or between the verb and the adverb.

**Examples**:

| | |
|---|---|
| อาหารไม่เผ็ด | *The food is not spicy.* |
| บ้านไม่สะอาด | *The house is not clean.* |
| คุณร้องเพลงไม่เก่ง | *You are not good at singing.* |
| ดิฉันขับรถไม่เร็ว | *I don't drive fast.* |
| เค้าพูดไม่ชัด | *He/She doesn't speak clearly.* |

## COMPREHENSION EXERCISES

### A. What are the English equivalents?

1. พวกเค้ามีบ้าน
2. เรามีรถ
3. ผมจะไปทำงาน
4. ใครจะมาที่นี่?
5. คุณทำงานอะไร?
6. คุณจะไปที่ไหน?
7. เราจะอยู่ที่นี่
8. เค้าอยู่ที่นั่น
9. เค้าอยู่ที่ไหน?
10. คุณจะไปที่นั่น
11. คุณจะไปที่นั่นรึเปล่า?
12. คุณจะไปที่นั่นใช่มั้ย?
13. คุณจะไปที่นั่นเมื่อไร?
14. ทำไมคุณจะไปที่นั่น?
15. ใครจะไปที่นั่น?
16. ที่นี่ร้อนมาก
17. เค้าทำงานเก่ง
18. เค้าทำงานไม่เก่ง
19. ทำไมเค้าไม่ไปทำงาน?
20. เค้ากินอาหารแล้วรึยัง?
21. เค้าเคยกินอาหารไทยแล้วรึยัง?
22. คุณกินอาหารเผ็ดได้มั้ย?
23. เค้ามีลูกกี่คน?
24. คุณเคยเห็นเค้ามั้ย?

25. คุณจะไปประเทศจีนเมื่อไร?

26. เค้ามาแล้วหรือยัง?

27. ทำไมเค้ายังไม่มา?

28. เค้าไปพัทยากับใคร?

29. วันนี้คุณพ่อมาไม่ได้

30. วันนี้คุณพ่อไม่ได้มา

31. รถเค้าสวยมาก

32. ดิฉันขับรถไม่เร็วมาก

## B. What are the Thai equivalents?

1. His home.

2. His home is big.

3. Is his home big?

4. I saw you.

5. What did you see?

6. Thailand is hot.

7. Thailand is not cold.

8. Small country.

9. He goes to work.

10. How does he go to work?

11. They are cold.

12. They are not hot.

13. Are you cold?

14. When will you go to Chiang Mai?

15. Why don't you like this job?

16. Why don't you drive?

17. What color do you like?
18. Which one is your friend?
19. Where did you park?
20. What is on the table?
21. My wife does not cook well.
22. Can you speak Chinese?
23. Have you eaten already?
24. Have you ever been to Australia?
25. You are cold, aren't you?
26. How many computers do you have?
27. I have four kids.
28. She is very hungry, isn't she?
29. This country is very beautiful.
30. The room is very small.
31. The house is not big.
32. He speaks fast.
33. I didn't play with him.
34. Can you write?
35. I can't read.

## C. Read the article and answer the questions.

คุณซูซานมาจากประเทศอิตาลี่ เค้า ชอบมาเที่ยวที่ประเทศไทยกับ เพื่อนชื่อ แซม คุณซูซานอยากมาทำงานที่กรุงเทพ เพราะว่า ที่นี่ ไม่หนาว อาหารอร่อย และของไม่แพง

1.  Where is Susan from?

    _____

2.  Where does she like to go on holiday?

    _____

3.  What is her friend's name?

    _____

4.  Where does she like to work?

    _____

5.  Why?

    _____

## D. Read the answers and create the corresponding questions.

1.  _____

    ผมเป็นคนไทย

2.  _____

    ผมทำงานที่กรุงเทพ

3. _____

ผมเป็นครู

4. _____

ผมชอบสอน

5. _____

ผมเดินไปทำงาน

6. _____

ผมขับรถไม่เป็น

7. _____

ผมไม่เคยไปภูเก็ต

8. _____

ผมจะไปภูเก็ตเดือนหน้า

9. _____

ผมมีลูกสองคน

10. _____

ลูกคนโตชื่อแดง คนเล็กชื่อดำ

## E. Use the given words to make correct sentences.

1. เพื่อน    ผม    มาก    เก่ง

2. กิน    ไทย    ผม    ชอบ    อาหาร

3. คอย    นาน    อยาก    ไม่

4. ใคร    ห้อง    ใน    อยู่

5. เด็ก    โรงเรียน    ทุก    ไป    วัน

6. ขวด    ขอ    น้ำ    หนึ่ง

7. ไม่    เช็ด    สะอาด    โต๊ะ

8. ดิฉัน    หิว    ลูก    มาก

9. เกาะ    ไกล    อยู่    ไม่

10. เค็ม    ไก่    มาก    ทอด

11. เก่า    แพง    ไม่    รถ

12. อะไร    คุณ    ทำ    ชอบ

# PART 3

# KEYS TO EXERCISES

## PART 1

**LESSON 1** - -

**LESSON 2** Consonants

A. 1. ก          2. ข ค ฆ          3. ง          4. จ

   5. ช ฉ ฌ      6. ซ ส ศ ษ        7. ย ญ        8. ด ฎ

   9. ต ฏ        10. ท ธ ฑ ฒ ถ ฐ   11. น ณ       12. บ

   13. ป         14. พ ผ ภ          15. ฟ ฝ       16. ม

   17. ร         18. ล ฬ            19. ว         20. ห ฮ

   21. อ

B. 1. ก ข ค ฆ

   2. ท ฒ ธ ถ ฐ จ ฉ  ช ฌ ศ ส ซ ด ต  ฏ ฎ ฑ ณ

   3. พ ภ  บ ป ฟ          4. ม

   5. น ณ ญ ร ล ฬ         6. ง

   7. ย                   8. ว

C. 1. a) มา        2. a) โท        3. b) ดี        4. a) แค่

   5. a) พอ        6. b) ปู         7. b) ใบ        8. b) โดน

   9. b) ธง        10. a) นาน

D. 1. a) มาก       2. a) โทษ       3. b) ตี         4. a) แคบ

   5. a) พอง       6. b) ปูด        7. b) ปาก        8. a) ทน

   9. b) ดม        10. b) งาน

**LESSON 3** Vowels

A. 1. ◌ั◌ , ◌ิ , ◌ี , ◌ื , ◌ือ

2. $\overset{\shortmid}{\underset{\text{ุ}}{\phantom{i}}}$ , $\overset{\shortmid}{\underset{\text{ู}}{\phantom{i}}}$

3. เ_ , แ_ , โ_ , ไ_ , ไ_

4. _ะ , _า , _อ

5. เ_ะ , แ_ะ , เ_าะ , เ_า , เ_อ , เ_อะ , โ_ะ

6. _ัว , _ัวะ , _ำ , เ_ือ

7. _ะ        to        _ _

   โ_ะ        to        _ _

   เ_ือ        to        เ_ือ

   เ_ะ        to        เ_ _

   แ_ะ        to        แ_ _

   เ_อ        to        เ_ _

   _ัว        to        _ว_

B. 1. เ_ะ       2. เ_       3. _ำ

    4. _ี       5. _ะ       6. _ื

    7. _ุ       8. เ_ือ       9. _ุ

    10. _า       11. ไ_       12. ไ_

    13. โ_       14. แ_ะ       15. แ_

    16. เ_ือ       17. _ัว       18. โ_

    19. เ_อ       20. _ี       21. _ัว

    22. เ_อ       23. เ_าะ       24. โ_ะ

    25. เ_ีย       26. เ_า       27. เ_อะ

    28. เ_อ       29. _ื       30. _ัว

    31. _อ       32. เ_ีย       33. เ_า

    34. _ำ       35. _ะ       36. _ัว

    37. _ี       38. _อ       39. เ_ะ

    40. _ัว

C.

| Word | Initial Consonant | Vowel | Final Consonant |
|------|-------------------|-------|-----------------|
| เดือน <br> *month* | ด | เ◌ือ | น |
| วัน <br> *day* | ว | ◌ั | น |
| ปี <br> *year* | ป | ◌ี | |
| นาน <br> *long time* | น | ◌า | น |
| เห็น <br> *to see* | ห | เ◌็ | น |
| รวม <br> *to include* | ร | ◌ัว | ม |
| หัว <br> *head* | ห | ◌ัว | |
| เดิน <br> *to walk* | ด | เ◌ิ | น |
| บน <br> *on* | บ | โ◌ะ | น |
| บอก <br> *to tell* | บ | ◌อ | ก |

| เขียน<br>*to write* | ข | เ ◌ ี ย | น |
|---|---|---|---|
| อ่าน<br>*to read* | อ | ◌ า | น |

D.  1. a) กิน       2. b) ใจ       3. c) ดึก

4. a) ตาย       5. a) บน       6. c) เปิด

7. b) อีก       8. c) เดียว       9. a) ปิด

10. c) จอด       11. c) ขน       12. b) สอด

E.  1. a       2. l       3. i       4.  h

5. k       6. c       7. n       8. m

9. b       10. f       11. g       12. j

13. d       14. e

F.  1. ◌ะ       ประ   ตั้ง   จะ   กลับ   ประ

2. ◌า       ลาว   ย้าย   มา   อา   อา   สาม   งาน   ลาว   หน้า

3. ◌ุ       ยุ   ยุ

4. ◌ู       อยู่

5. ไ◌       ไทย   ไป

6. แ◌ะ       และ

7. แ◌       แต่   แล้ว

8. เ◌า       เก้า

9. โ◌ะ       ผม   ผม   ผม   ผม   ผม   ผม   จบ

10. เ◌ือ       เมือง   เดือน

11. ◌ื อ       ชื่อ

12. ◌ำ       ดำ   ทำ

13. เ◌อ       เกิด   เพิ่ง

14. เ_ีย  เรียน

15. _ิ  สิบ

16. _ี  ที่  ที  นี้  ยี่  ปี  ที่

17. เ_  เทศ  เทศ

18. _อ  ครอบ ตอน

19. _ัว  ครัว  ขวบ

## LESSON 4  Initial Consonants

A. 1. ข      ย      ฟ      ศ      ค      ท
   2. ม      ร      จ      พ      ว
   3. ล      อ
   4. -

B. 1. A    2. D    3. F    4. E    5. G    6. B    7. C

C. 1. G    2. E    3. A    4. D    5. B    6. C    7. F

## LESSON 5  Final Consonants

A. 1. ง      2. ม      3. น      4. ณ      5. ญ      6. ร      7. ล
   8. พ      9. ย      10. ว

B.   น,      ณ,      ญ,      ร,      ล,      พ

C. 1. ก,      ข,      ค,      ฆ

   2. ด,      ฎ,      จ,      ฉ,      ช,      ฌ,      ซ,      ฐ,      ถ,

      ต,      ฏ,      ท,      ธ,      ฑ,      ฒ,      ษ,      ศ,      ส

   3. บ,      ป,      พ,      ภ,      ฟ

D. 1. A    2. A    3. B    4. B    5. A    6. A    7. A    8. A
   9. A    10. A   11. B   12. B   13. B   14. A   15. A

E. 1. B    2. A    3. B    4. B    5. A    6. A    7. A    8. B
9. A    10. A    11. B    12. A    13. B    14. A    15. A

F.

| ก<br>g-1, k-stop | ข<br>k-2, k-stop | ค<br>k-3, k-stop | ฆ<br>k-3, k-stop | ง<br>ng-4, ng-son. |
|---|---|---|---|---|
| จ<br>j-1, t-stop | ฉ<br>ch-2, t-stop | ช<br>ch-3, t-stop | ซ<br>s-3, t-stop | ฌ<br>ch-3, t-stop |
| ญ<br>y-4, n-son. | ฎ<br>d-1, t-stop | ฏ<br>dt-1, t-stop | ฐ<br>t-2, t-stop | ฑ<br>t-3, t-stop |
| ฒ<br>t-3, t-stop | ณ<br>n-4, n-son. | ด<br>d-1, t-stop | ต<br>dt-1, t-stop | ถ<br>t-2, t-stop |
| ท<br>t-3, t-stop | ธ<br>t-3, t-stop | น<br>n-4, n-son. | บ<br>b-1, p-stop | ป<br>bp-1, p-stop |
| ผ<br>p-2, - | ฝ<br>f-2, - | พ<br>p-3, p-stop | ฟ<br>f-3, p-stop | ภ<br>p-3, p-stop |
| ม<br>m-4,m-son. | ย<br>y-4, y, ii-son. | ร<br>r-4, n-son. | ล<br>l-4, n-son. | ว<br>w-4, oo-son. |
| ศ<br>s-2, t-stop | ษ<br>s-2, t-stop | ส<br>s-2, t-stop | ห<br>h-2, - | ฬ<br>l-4, n-son. |
| อ<br>-1, - | ฮ<br>h-3, - | | | |

G. 1. G    2. J    3. H    4. O    5. L    6. B    7. K    8. N
9. M    10. F    11. C    12. I    13. D    14. A    15. E

**LESSON 6** Tones

A.
| | | |
|---|---|---|
| 1. mid | 2. mid | 3. falling |
| 4. low | 5. mid | 6. low |
| 7. mid-mid | 8. rising | 9. low |
| 10. mid | 11. falling | 12. low |
| 13. falling | 14. mid | 15. low |
| 16. low-mid | 17. low | 18. falling |
| 19. low | 20. mid | 21. mid |
| 22. low | 23. low | 24. low |
| 25. low | 26. mid-mid | 27. low |
| 28. high-mid | 29. falling | 30. low |

B.
| | |
|---|---|
| 1. falling rising rising | 2. mid low |
| 3. rising low | 4. rising rising |
| 5. rising-rising | 6. rising rising |
| 7. rising | 8. rising mid mid |
| 9. rising falling | 10. falling low |
| 11. falling falling | 12. falling mid |
| 13. falling mid low | 14. falling rising |
| 15. mid rising low | 16. rising mid low |
| 17. low mid | |

C.
| | |
|---|---|
| 1. falling-rising | 2. mid high |
| 3. mid-rising | 4. mid-high |
| 5. mid-falling | 6. mid-rising |
| 7. high falling low | 8. mid falling rising |
| 9. high high | 10. low high |
| 11. falling low low-low | 12. falling-low-high |

13. falling low high        14. high mid

15. low-mid        16. mid high

17. falling mid        18. mid-high-mid

D.  1. a-b    2. a-c    3. a-b    4. a-c    5. a-b

6. a-c    7. b-c    8. a-b    9. a-b    10. a-b

E.

| | Words | | Initial Cons. | Vowel | Final Cons. | Tone |
|---|---|---|---|---|---|---|
| 1. | กับ | with | ก | _ ะ | บ | Low |
| 2. | ยุ่ง | busy | ย | ◌ุ | ง | Falling |
| 3. | ลื่น | slippery | ล | ◌ื_ | น | Falling |
| 4. | วัด | temple | ว | _ ะ | ด | High |
| 5. | เดือน | month | ด | เ◌ือ | น | Mid |
| 6. | เดิน | to walk | ด | เ◌อ | น | Mid |
| 7. | เพื่อน | friend | พ | เ◌ือ | น | Falling |
| 8. | กิน | to eat | ก | ◌ิ | น | Mid |
| 9. | ถูก | cheap | ถ | ◌ู | ก | Low |
| 10. | แพง | expensive | พ | แ_ | ง | Mid |
| 11. | โมง | o'clock | ม | โ_ | ง | Mid |
| 12. | ร้าน | shop | ร | _า | น | High |
| 13. | สี | color | ส | ◌ี | - | Rising |
| 14. | เขียน | to write | ข | เ◌ีย | น | Rising |
| 15. | น้ำ | water | น | _ำ | - | High |
| 16. | ด้วย | too | ด | ◌ัว | ย | Falling |
| 17. | ต้อง | must | ต | _อ | ง | Falling |

**LESSON 7** The Key Four 'อ' Words    --

**LESSON 8** How to Read Groups of Words

A. 1. ฉัน    ไม่    รู้
   2. สี    ไม่    สวย
   3. เต็ม    แล้ว
   4. ถูก    และ    ดี
   5. จอด    รถ    ใน    บ้าน
   6. พี่    ชาย    คุณ
   7. ลูก    สาว    ผม    ชื่อ    เล็ก
   8. คุณ    พ่อ    ไม่    ดื่ม    เบียร์
   9. อ่าน    ได้    แต่    เขียน    ไม่    ได้
   10. คุณ    แดง    จะ    ไป    หา    หมอ
   11. คุณ    จะ    ไป    กี่    โมง
   12. เลี้ยว    ซ้าย    ที่    สี่    แยก

B. ตอน/ ผม/ เป็น/ เด็ก/ ผม/ ชอบ/ เรียน/ ภา-ษา/ จีน/ มาก/ ที่-สุด/ แต่/ เพื่อน/ หลาย/ คน/ ไม่/ ชอบ/ ภา-ษา/ นี้/ บาง/ คน/ บอก/ ว่า/ ภา-ษา/จีน/ ยาก/ มาก/ บาง/ คน/ บอก/ ว่า/ ชอบ/ ภา-ษา/ อื่น/ แล้ว/ คุณ/ ล่ะ/ ชอบ/ ภา-ษา/ อะ-ไร/ มาก/ ที่-สุด

C. 1. เรียน    2. เพื่อน    3. หลาย    4. ยาก
   5. ภาษา    6. ชอบ    7. บาง    8. อะไร
   9. แต่    10. ไม่    11. มาก    12. บอก

**LESSON 9** Irregular Phonetics    --

**LESSON 10** Two Initial Consonants

A. 1. b    2. a    3. a    4. a    5. b

B. 1. จะ-หมูก                   2. ตะ-หลาด

    3. ปล่อย                   4. อะ-หร่อย

    5. ขะ-หนาด               6. ขะ-หยัน

    7. สะ-หนุก                8. สะ-หนาม

    9. ฉะ-หลอง              10. ถะ-หนน

    11. พะ-แนง               12. ถะ-แหลง

    13. ผะ-เด็ด-กาน         14. สะ-เหลด

    15. สะ-โหร่ง             16. สะ-เหนอ

    17. ผะ-แหนก            18. จะ-เริน

    19. ฉะ-หลาม            20. ขะ-เหมน

**LESSON 11** Pronunciation Irregularities --

**LESSON 12** Rules of 'ร'

A. 1. เรา จะ สร้าง ที่-ทำ-งาน ใหม่

    2. เรา ทำ-งาน เสร็จ แล้ว

    3. หาด-ทราย ที่-นี่ สวย มาก

    4. ธรรมดา ทหาร ชอบ มา ที่-นี่

    5. ไม่ ทราบ ค่ะ

B. 1. falling    2. low    3. mid

    4. high    5. falling    6. falling

**LESSON 13** Miscellaneous Signs --

**LESSON 14**   Silent Vowels Consonants

A.  1. ญาติ (*relatives*)          2. สามารถ (*to be able to*)
    3. สมัคร (*to apply*)          4. เกษตร (*agriculture*)
    5. ชาติ (*nation*)

**LESSON 15**  About ฤ      --

**LESSON 16**  Unusual Spellings      --

**LESSON 17**  Twenty 'ใ' Thai Words

A.  1. ใบ้        2. ใน        3. ใต้        4. ใหญ่
    5. ใช่        6. ใบ        7. ใช้        8. ให้
    9. ใคร      10. ใกล้      11. ใส        12. ใจ

**LESSON 18**   Words of Similar Pronunciation

A.  1. a)    2. b)    3. a)    4. b)    5. b)    6. b)    7. a)

**LESSON 19**   Main Vocabulary Lists

A.  1. จะ        2. ขา        3. สิบ        4. รีบ
    5. ดึง        6. มืด        7. อายุ        8. ถูก
    9. เตะ      10. ประเทศ   11. แข็ง       12. รถ
   13. โสด      14. เกาะ      15. ขอ        16. เยอะ
   17. เจอ      18. เสีย      19. เพื่อน      20. กลัว
   21. ทำ       22. ใน       23. ไฟ        24. ภูเขา

**LESSON 20**   Additional Useful Vocabulary   --

## LESSON 21   Menus, Forms, Labels, Signs

A.  1. ต้มยำไก่
    2. แกงเขียวหวานหมู
    3. ยำเนื้อ
    4. กุ้งทอด
    5. ก๋วยเตี๋ยวทะเล
    6. ไข่เจียวไก่สับ
    7. ผัดผักคะน้าน้ำมันหอย
    8. หมูย่าง
    9. น้ำส้ม (คั้น)
    10. ชาเย็น

B.  1. Plastic
    2. Mansion
    3. Microphone
    4. Motorcycle
    5. Fax
    6. Sofa
    7. Apartment
    8. Condominium
    9. Computer
    10. Video
    11. Poster
    12. Air (Conditioner)
    13. Tape
    14. CD
    15. Tractor
    16. Board
    17. Cartoon
    18. Cutter
    19. Shampoo
    20. Digital

C.  1. Cheese Sandwiches
    2. Salad
    3. Macaroni
    4. Ham Sandwiches
    5. Pizza
    6. Soup
    7. Hamburger
    8. Pasta
    9. Spaghetti
    10. Lasagna
    11. Bacon
    12. French Fries
    13. Hotdog
    14. Ice-cream
    15. Cake
    16. Cookie
    17. Chocolate
    18. Beer
    19. Wine
    20. Pepsi

D. 1. b   2. a   3. b   4. b   5. a   6. b   7. a   8. a

## LESSON 22  Calendar and Geography

A.  1. วันขึ้นปีใหม่

2. เมษายน        มิถุนายน        กันยายน        พฤศจิกายน

3. มกราคม        มีนาคม        พฤษภาคม        กรกฎาคม
   สิงหาคม        ตุลาคม        ธันวาคม

4. กุมภาพันธ์

5. เมษายน

6. ธันวาคม

7. 5 ธันวาคม

8. 12 สิงหาคม

9. กุมภาพันธ์

B.  1. Australia

2. Malaysia

3. Spain

4. Russia

5. Italy

6. Colombia

7. Chili

8. America

9. Brunei

10. Iraq

11. Sudan

12. Singapore

13. Vietnam

14. Canada

15. India

**LESSON 23**   Questions, Games, Crosswords

A. 1. b   2. f   3. d   4. i   5. d   6. g   7. c   8. e   9. a   10. j

B. 1. b   2. a   3. c   4. b   5. b   6. c   7. b   8. b   9. a

C. 1. จอง          2. จาน          3. อาหาร          4. งาน

   5. ตลาด       6. จอด          7. หมา          8. รถ

   9. ทอด       10. ถาม         11. นาน         12. ตอบ

D. 1. g   2. i   3. h   4. b   5. d   6. e   7. f   8. c   9. a   10. l   11. j   12. k

E. 1. c   2. b   3. h   4. f   5. g   6. i   7. j   8. e   9. d   10. a   11. l   12. k

F. 1. d   2. c   3. g   4. b   5. i   6. h   7. f   8. j   9. a   10. e

G. 1. c   2. a   3. b   4. c   5. a   6. a   7. a   8. a   9. b   10. a

H.

I.

| | | ¹ชี้ | ²อ | | | | | | | |
| | | | อ | | | ⁴บ | | | | |
| ³พ | ว | ก | เ | ร | า | | | | | |
| | | | จ | | ⁵ย | า | ⁶ก | | | |
| | | | า | | | | ร | | ¹³ท | |
| | | ¹¹ก | ¹²ล้ | ว | ย | | ะ | | า | |
| | | | า | | | | ¹⁴โ | ม | ง | |
| ¹⁵ที่ | ไ | ห | น | | | | ป | | | |
| | | | | | | | ร | | | |
| | | | | | | ⁷ง | า | ⁸น | | |
| | | | | | | | | ว | | |
| | | | | | | ⁹ป | ว | ด | | |
| | | | | | | | | เ | | |
| | | | | | | | | ท้ | | |
| | | | | | | ¹⁰ห | ม | า | | |

J.

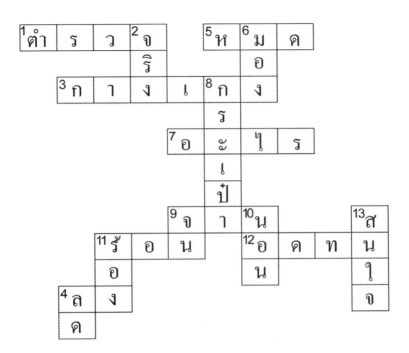

K.  1. อะไร      2. ที่ไหน      3. เมื่อไร      4. ทำไม

      5. เท่าไร      6. อาหาร      7. สบายดี      8. เห็น

      9. ข้าว      10. ถูก      11. แพง      12. ชอบ

      13. เพื่อน      14. เผ็ด      15. ร้อน      16. นัด

      17. สาย      18. เจอ      19. อยู่

## PART 2

**LESSON 24**  How to Form Phrases and Sentences

A.  1. They have a house/houses.

    2. We have a car/cars.

    3. I am going to/will go to work.

    4. Who is coming/will come here?

    5. What do you do (for a living?)

    6. Where are you going?

    7. We will stay here.

    8. He/she is there.

    9. Where is he/she?

    10. You are going there.

    11. Are you going there?

    12. You're going there, aren't you?

    13. When are you going there?

    14. Why are you going there?

    15. Who is going there?

    16. It's very hot here.

    17. He/she is good at his/her work.

    18. He/she is not good at his/her work.

19. Why doesn't he/she go to work?

20. Has he/she eaten yet?

21. Has he/she ever had Thai food before?

22. Can you eat spicy food?

23. How many children does he/she have?

24. Have you ever seen him before?

25. When are you going to China?

26. Has he/she come yet?

27. Why hasn't he/she come yet?

28. Who did he/she go to Pattaya with?

29. Father can not come today.

30. Father did not come today.

31. His/her car is very beautiful.

32. I don't drive very fast.

B.  1. บ้าน(ของ)เขา

2. บ้าน(ของ)เขาใหญ่

3. บ้าน(ของ)เขาใหญ่ไหม?

4. ผม(ดิฉัน)เห็นคุณ

5. คุณเห็นอะไร?

6. ประเทศไทยร้อน

7. ประเทศไทยไม่หนาว

8. ประเทศเล็ก

9. เขาไปทำงาน

10. เขาไปทำงานยังไง?

11. พวกเขาหนาว

12. พวกเขาไม่ร้อน

13. คุณหนาวไหม?

14. คุณจะไปเชียงใหม่เมื่อไร?

15. ทำไมคุณไม่ชอบงานนี้ ?

16. ทำไมคุณไม่ขับรถ ?

17. คุณชอบสีอะไร?

18. เพื่อนคุณคนไหน? OR คนไหนเพื่อนคุณ?

19. คุณจอดรถที่ไหน?

20. อะไรอยู่บนโต๊ะ?

21. ภรรยาผมทำอาหารไม่เก่ง

22. คุณพูดภาษาจีนได้ไหม?

23. คุณกินข้าวแล้วหรือยัง?

24. คุณเคยไปออสเตรเลียแล้วหรือยัง?

25. คุณหนาวใช่ไหม?

26. คุณมีคอมพิวเตอร์กี่เครื่อง?

27. ผมมีลูกสี่คน

28. เขาหิวมากใช่ไหม?

29. ประเทศนี้สวยมาก

30. ห้องเล็กมาก

31 บ้านไม่ใหญ่

32. เขาพูดเร็ว

33. ผมไม่ได้เล่นกับเขา

34. คุณเขียนได้ไหม?

35. ผมอ่านไม่ได้

C. 1. Italy    2. Thailand    3. Sam    4. Bangkok

5. Because Bangkok is not cold, has delicious food and is not expensive.

D.  1. คุณเป็นคนอะไร?                2. คุณทำงานที่ไหน?
    3. คุณทำงานอะไร?                4. คุณชอบทำอะไร?
    5. คุณไปทำงานอย่างไร?           6. คุณขับรถเป็นไหม?
    7. คุณเคยไปภูเก็ตไหม?            8. คุณจะไปภูเก็ตเมื่อไหร?
    9. คุณมีลูกกี่คน?               10. ลูกคุณชื่ออะไร?

E.  1. เพื่อนผมเก่งมาก              2. ผมชอบกินอาหารไทย
    3. ไม่อยากคอยนาน               4. ใครอยู่ในห้อง?
    5. เด็กไปโรงเรียนทุกวัน          6. ขอน้ำหนึ่งขวด
    7. เช็ดโต๊ะไม่สะอาด             8. ลูกดิฉันหิวมาก
    9. เกาะอยู่ไม่ไกล              10. ไก่ทอดเค็มมาก
   11. รถเก่าไม่แพง               12. คุณชอบทำอะไร?